BPI PROUDLY PRESENTS

THE FORMULA

A MAJOR IMPROVEMENT TO THE DESIGN OF OUR LIVES

Produced by Bandit Publishing Inc.

Copyright © 2010 By Bintell Powell, Library of Congress

ISBN: 978-0-578-05690-6

Single copies may be ordered via info@banditpublishing.net or by contacting Bintell Powell via ISBN above. Quantity discounts are also available. In your e-mail transmittal, include information concerning the intended number of books you wish to purchase.

Printed in Canada

*W*hat a glorious thought. A formula that all people can use to become as successful as they ever dreamed they could be; as successful as you want to be. It's heartwarming to know that now, with the use of The Formula, you can free yourself from financial insecurity, no matter who you are, or where you come from.

Peace of mind and security are waiting for you in the arms of The Formula. It is here to protect you from financial hopelessness like a soft warm blanket protects you from the cold. Relax, take a deep breath and allow yourself to breathe a sigh of relief. Success is on the way.

The answers to all our social and financial failures have been right in front of us the whole time. This book is simply making it visible to the world. It's been on the tip of every person's tongue I have ever talked to and now, success has a name and an address.

Here is exactly what The Formula is going to do for you:

The Formula will...

- Show you that success is a simple choice
- Teach you how to get success to chase after you
- Show you how easy it is to take pain and failure, and create wild success
- Turn you into a company unto yourself
- Turn you into the best President and CEO ever
- Show you how to use your passion, talent and genius to make yourself rich
- Turn you into a Master in any area
- Tell you why attending college is the best way to get your hands on The Formula
- Show you how to guarantee your success

THE FORMULA IS:

SUCCESS FILTERED DOWN TO ITS BAREST ESSENTIALS.

A HOMEMADE APPLIANCE FOR THE ART OF MANUFACTURING MONEY.

A MAJOR IMPROVEMENT TO THE SOCIAL & FINANCIAL DESIGN OF OUR LIVES...

A MONEY REVOLUTION!

Information

Relationships

Commodities

MAKES SUCCESS NO LONGER AN AMERICAN DREAM, NOW IT'S A WORLD-WIDE REALITY!!!

YOUR PERSONAL PHD IN MONEY

IT'S SIMPLE...
IT'S TESTED...
IT WORKS!!!

ACKNOWLEDGMENTS

There are so many people I have to thank for this project finally becoming a reality. First and foremost, I have to thank my entire family who has stood by me through all the ups and downs of my ever so rocky and painful professional career. I could NEVER have done this without you.

Thanks to my loving mother who sacrificed so much for me. Thanks to my father who forced me to face all the pain and suffering in the world. Thanks to my sister who is an inspiration to our entire family.

To my daughter, thank you for inspiring me to leave a tool behind for you that will act as a foundation for all the social and financial success you will find when I am no longer here to protect you. Your life is an occasion my love. Use this Formula and rise to it. I will be watching you, rooting for you every step of the way, pass or fail.

Thanks to my long time friend and editor, Beverley Wilson for going through this book with a fine tooth comb over, and over, and over. If nothing else, this project is proof of the value of relationships and cooperative effort. I could never have done this without you!

Thanks to all those managers I have worked for that shaped my business personality one job at a time. Each one of you, good or bad, have helped me to recognize this formula through each success and failure we experienced.

Thank you Mr. Neil White for that poem you gave me for my first book. It inspires me to this very day. If not for our heartfelt conversations many a late night, this contribution to society may never have been. You said, "Success is a point in time where preparation and opportunity collide." Impressed and inspired by the truth of your statement, this formula spilled out of my mouth. We both sat there stunned, realizing that against the odds, I may have actually stumbled upon something that could have a positive impact on the lives of many. Let us see if we were right.

Thanks to Rich Chereskin for hiring me when nobody else would give me a chance. Thanks for giving me a fully functional money machine to play with way back then. Had I known what I know now, I would not have spent 20 years searching for it. I would have realized that you had already given it to me.

And last but certainly not least, thanks to all the people that will use this formula to make all their dreams come true. Nothing would make me happier than to see you achieve all that you deserve in this life, and much, much more. I'll be watching you, rooting for you to break new success records. Know your human right. Use The Formula and be what you come here for!

May you be forever blessed in everything, and anything you do!

SUCCESS IS:

**SOMETHING THAT TURNS OUT
AS PLANNED**

**A POINT IN TIME WHERE
PREPARATION AND
OPPORTUNITY COLLIDE**

**THE ATTAINMENT OF WEALTH,
FAME & POWER**

SUCCESS IS A CHOICE!

CONTENTS

❧

ACT ONE

Success = Information + Commodities + Relationships = $$$

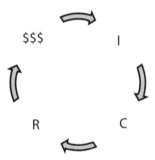

$$$

I

R

C

COULD IT BE?

WHAT IF?

☙

SUCCESS IS THE ATTAINMENT OF WEALTH, FAME AND POWER.

What if there could ever really be a simple and easy to use formula for financial success? What if everything you needed for this formula to produce tons of money, was patiently waiting for you to reach out and simply grab it? Suppose it was free and available to everyone, every second, of everyday?

As a child I heard adults talk about a "mystical magical formula for success" as if it was more valuable than even the Bible. But if it was real, and simple, I mean so simple a child could use it, it would change the social and financial worlds of those that desperately need it--forever.

Making money would suddenly be like gambling with a fixed deck of cards, or scoring 100% on a difficult test with a cheat sheet. We could use this formula to predict what success will do next and then, just sit back and watch our success play out. A formula for success would be like giving the entire world, a VIP pass to the good life.

The truth is, success formulas are already a big part of our lives. We take them for granted, although we are slaves to the way they reliably predict success' behavior for us. Being an engineer, I call them formulas, while others call them behavioral models, because they show us exactly how to behave successfully. Without them, the seven billion people of the

> *A model is an example of success*

3

world would not know how to behave, from one minute to the next.

Fashion models teach us how to dress for success. An athletic coach's playbook is full of formulas for success in his/her chosen sport. Church is a formula for spiritual success. Financial people have tons of formulas and business models they secretly use to make themselves millions, sometimes even billions of dollars every year.

The explosion of reality shows on television is purely because they teach us how and how not to behave in various situations. My daughter at just five years of age, wants to dress and act exactly like Cinderella. She sleeps with her Cinderella doll as if they are best friends. If I want to stop her from behaving a certain way, I will say, "Cinderella would not behave like that, now would she?" It stops her in her tracks every time.

The great psychologist Abraham Maslow gave us a model for predicting human behavior. The OSI Model is a formula for the predictable behavior of computers and the Internet. It is largely responsible for turning Bill Gates into one of the richest men on Earth. The legendary Henry Ford created a formula for mass-producing affordable cars, giving birth to a World Wide Automotive Industry. The car he produced with that formula was of all things called, The Model T.

Come to think of it, my entire college career was filled with formulas and models designed to successfully predict the behavior of electricity, and then manipulate its power. There are even successful people we call role models, that young and old look up to and imitate their behavior to the letter. Leading psychologist will tell you, people perform best when they are imitating models.

Successful business people know how you behave and they have put your behavior into formulas that allow them to successfully capture large amounts of your money. They can turn economic failure, into economic super power, as hard-working people look on confused and amazed, clueless to the fact that a secret formula is being used to ensure the financial success of these super successful people.

Their secret success formulas are designed to do one thing, which is to guarantee their success with the smallest amount of risk for failure. Successful people avoid risk like the plague. They know all too well that there is no better way to avoid the risk of failure, than to use a formula for success. If they do not make a certain amount of money using one, they will say, "Okay, this formula is not working anymore. That means the behavior of our customer has changed so, we are going to need a new formula."

When times are good and jobs with steady paychecks are the norm, we allow ourselves to believe the success formula of blindly going to college for as long as you can afford, and then praying to God that you land a high paying job actually works. Although higher education is an infinitely valuable tool and very effective for those that understand how to apply it, this model of behavior can be ineffective for many.

> *1% of the world's people control more than 50% of the world's wealth*

This success formula is not solely designed to help you make lots of money. It is a commodity for sale designed to also keep you in debt and stuck working in the rat race forever. Why you ask? Well, the answer is a simple one. Those who control the debt, then control the interest, the profit and thus, the world.

Unfortunately, millions of us blindly rely on the success formula of college + job = success, like a crippled man relies on his crutch. But soon our worlds are turned upside down with recessions, corporate mergers and downsizing, leaving us addicted to unemployment and forced to deal with the reality that, when we need a success formula for making money the most, we have nothing.

There is an alternative to all this failure. I watched a single mother, in less than a year, go from being a clerk, to a partner in a law firm making half a million dollars each year. I have also witnessed people from near poverty use this formula to become multi-millionaires. Ultra successful people know all too well that the individual with the most behavioral models and success formulas for making money will win in this game of wealth, fame and power.

The top nine percent with *The Formula* firmly in their grasp have you in an almost impossible position. You are stuck in the dreaded rat race, in debt, with financial responsibilities up to your eyeballs. As a result, you will continue to chase a paycheck, risking heart attack and worse, precious time forever lost without seeing your children and loved ones.

Successful people have power over you for one reason. You do not have *The Formula* and the only way you will ever be able to defend yourself against them, is if you get your hands on it, and master its use.

After years of living with no direction, being tossed around like a rag doll by the rat race, hoping financial success would somehow land in my lap, I was finally able to grab the success I had dreamed of for years using this formula. Having it and not having it was like day and night.

Like a race car tuned to perfection, this formula sped past everyone, lapping people still caught in the grips of the rat race as if they were standing still. The terrible irony about the pleasure of financial success we all seek is, it is built off of all the pain, confusion and misfortune of everyday people like you and me.

FORMULAS NEVER BREAK DOWN AND THEY ALWAYS WORK. THEY ARE THE MOST RELIABLE MACHINES KNOWN TO MAN. GOING THROUGH LIFE WITH NO SUCCESS FORMULA, IS A FORMULA FOR SURE FAILURE.

PAIN IS PROFIT

> *"I am always on the lookout for those good, simple solutions to everyday problems."*
> Martha Stewart

ℰℓ

IF YOU WANT THE PEOPLE OF THE WORLD TO GIVE YOU MILLIONS, PROVIDE THEM WITH RELIEF FROM THEIR ACHES AND PAINS.

The most important thing I learned all those years trapped in the rat race, working for that small group of people already using this formula is, the pain of the world, is profit for the rich and powerful.

After 20 years of sales training classes designed to arm me with the two most important formulas for success in sales, how to ask the right questions and then, how to listen so that you can understand a person's pain and make huge profit, it finally hit me.

The billions of people of this world live only to do one simple thing. That thing is to avoid at all cost, any and all unpleasant and painful situations on Earth. To do this, human beings use products.

From the moment we wake, until the time we close our eyes for sleep, staying clear of anything painful, and hopefully experiencing a bit of pleasure is the only thing we are really trying to do. Some will even tell you a full day of no pain at all, is itself a much-needed day of pure pleasure. An example of the thin line between products, pain and pleasure is, cigarettes provide short term pleasure from stress, yet long term pain through cancer.

With that in mind, the goal of all people looking to be financially successful is to take complicated and painful problems for people of all walks of life, and turn them into simple and easy to use products, that make life pleasant and heavenly for all.

Food protects us from hunger pains. Lawyers help their clients recover money for damages due to traumatic pain and suffering. Medicine protects us from pain of disease like aspirin saves us from the pain of a headache. Cars save us from the physical pain of walking for miles on end. Weather reporters save us from the painfully harsh elements of the world. Natural disasters within hours can put entire nations in so much pain, they are deemed a "state of emergency."

Entertainment like movies and music protects us from the emotional pain of being alone, bored, sad or worse, heartbroken. Knee pads, gloves, umbrellas, and homes are all designed to protect us from the physical pain of the world's harsh elements. Anyone who has ever invented anything was really trying to protect themselves from pain. Although they do not know it, the people who are at the so-called "bottom of society" are the richest people on Earth, as they have first hand access to the most pain in life. They are more valuable than they could ever imagine.

Legend has it that the international soft drink Coca Cola was discovered accidently. John S. Pemberton was really trying to come up with a tonic to relieve headaches mixing syrup in his three-legged kettle. The most famous motivational slogan in all of sports is, "No pain, no gain." Top athletes believe that pain is weakness leaving the body. In the armed forces, generals and captains will say, "Pain is your friend. It tells you if nothing else, you are still alive."

Whether it is a book, or a bicycle, medicine or even money itself, the purpose of all products is to make this world, a pain free place for everyone. Unfortunately, discomfort and pain are the tollbooths we all must go through as we enter, and leave this sweet and wonderfully majestic world we call Mother Earth.

Mothers must endure labor pains to give children life. A newborn baby cries in protest of its new environment that is suddenly unpleasant, compared to the blissfully comfortable womb of its mother. The fear of our loved ones experiencing or worse, passing on due to painful disease is a heartbreaking thought. Pain and discomfort, throughout life, in its many shapes and forms, is the greatest challenge to all mankind.

It could be a bandage, a paperclip or anesthesia, the end result is the same. Wild social and financial success is a result of the relief of pain a product will provide. Successful people take this a step further by using *The Formula* to turn their pain relieving products, into hot commodities, creating incredible profits for themselves.

No matter what anyone will ever tell you, success is a two-step process. Step one is to create pain relief, and step two is to sell it. If you want to make millions and billions, you have to wear one or both of these hats. If not, you are going to have to relieve a lot of pain for those that are.

CREATION AND SALES ARE THE CORNERSTONES OF WEALTH, FAME AND POWER.

THE DIFFERENCE

&

> *It is said that 91% of the people in this world are unknowingly funding the blissfully pain free lives of the top 9%*

"A BUSINESS IS SUCCESSFUL TO THE EXTENT THAT IT PROVIDES A PRODUCT OR SERVICE THAT CONTRIBUTES TO HAPPINESS IN ALL OF ITS FORMS."
   - MIHALY CSIKSZENTMIHALYI

The single difference between the working class and the ultra rich is this. Successful people embrace pain with open arms and then, they create a product to cure it. On the other hand, people teetering on the verge of financial destruction, living check-to-check, run frantically from pain, headlong into the pain relieving products of the rich, turning them into what successful people call, hot commodities.

Successful people understand that they can either create the product, or they can turn themselves into the product, or even better, a combination of the two. Because people buy things from people they trust, creating a product, and at the same time turning yourself into a trustworthy product you can sell in a package deal, is a social and economic slam dunk. *The Formula* is here to make this creating and selling stuff, simple and easy for everyone.

The big secret of all creation is, anything that people buy in large amounts that has ever, or ever will be created, started with the four little words, *"Instead of…what if?"* Whether it is a toothpick invented by a caveman, or a heat-seeking missile built by NASA Engineers, its creation began with those four little words. *Instead of...what if?*

Bill Gates, one of the top two richest men on Earth said, "*Instead of* memorizing all these long and boring commands needed to use a computer, *what if* we gave people pictures they could just click on instead? We would save people tons of time and energy memorizing all those painfully long commands, and make the world of computing a much simpler place." With that question, the world famous Microsoft Windows program was born.

A fifteen-year-old boy named Chester Greenwood in 1873 asked himself, "*Instead of* putting my hands over my ears when they get cold every 10 seconds, *what if* I take some cotton and some wire and let that protect my ears instead?" With that question, the earmuff was born.

Yes, it is actually as simple as it sounds. Still, because of the way engineers are trained to think, and because most people do not know this secret of creation, companies hire engineers to dream up products, and rely on salespeople to turn them into hot commodities, making the world for millions and billions of people, a wonderfully blissful pain free place. Although millions of people throughout the world are terrified of it, sales is even simpler than creation.

The secret of sales is in one word, **trust**. The bigger secret is, there are only three things needed to get people to trust in anything enough to buy it, and luckily, those three things are the three parts of *The Formula*. Why that is important to you is, salespeople make more money than anyone else on Earth.

In 2009, Best Buy named its new CEO Brian Dunn at age 49. Mr. Dunn started his career in 1985 at Best Buy selling televisions in their retail stores. Ray Kroc, the mastermind behind the most successful franchise ever, started off as a door-to-door milk shake machine salesman. Working this job, he found the idea for the most successful fast-food restaurant on Earth, McDonalds.

In any company, ANY job other than the engineer, and the salesperson are there to help the engineer make more products, and help the salespeople sell more of those same products. From the accountant, to the lawyer, to the receptionist, all the way over to the facilities manager and then right up to the president and CEO's office, they are ALL there to aid in the process of creating and selling. Although you may think your payroll manager is responsible for your paycheck, it is really the engineer and the salesmen you have to thank for them.

If only there was an easy way to show everyone how simple it is to dream up new and exciting products, and then sell them to billions of people throughout the world. If only there was a way to combine the engineer, and the salesman into one person. Turning the people of the world into Sales Engineers would truly be heaven sent. It would be like turning the world's people into money machines. It would be like giving the whole world a formula for success.

ALL OF HUMAN LIFE ON EARTH IS PEOPLE PROCESSING INFORMATION, AND THEN MAKING CHOICES TO AVOID PAIN. IF FINANCIAL SUCCESS IS YOUR GOAL, SOCIETIES CHOICE TO AVOID PAIN MUST INVOLVE A PRODUCT OWNED BY YOU.

ACT TWO

Success = Information + Commodities + Relationships = $$$

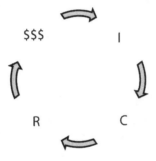

$$$ I

R C

THE MONEY MACHINE

SUCCESS = I + C + R

MONEY MACHINES FOR EVERYONE

∞

MONEY IS A REACTION TO SUCCESS, LIKE SWEATING IS A REACTION TO PHYSICAL ACTIVITY.

Nine percent of the world has tons of it. Ninety one percent of the world is dying to get their hands on just enough to survive. Money! Whenever conversations about it come up with associates and friends, I always joke and say, "When and if I ever go back to college, it will be for a PhD in Money." That little joke never fails to raise an eyebrow, a smile, or depending on the crowd, all out laughter.

As much time as we spend working hard for money, or talking about how much money we would love to have, our never ending saga of *making* money, and how much money we need for this and that, never once have I heard anybody say, "To make money, you need to mix paper, with pictures of famous faces, and then add a teaspoon of green ink, stir and place in the oven for an hour, and voila! There you have it. Piping hot money." It is either the people who have tons of it found it by chance and really do not know what it is made of, or they are just not telling us how they make so much of it.

At around nine years of age, the bickering over money in my home reached a fever pitch. Just as things were getting out of control, I managed to make what I felt was a major discovery about how money was really made. This discovery came right as my parents were having yet another argument over the mortgage.

There it was, on television as clear as day. A huge grey machine spitting out money faster than anything I had ever seen. There was no information on the bottom of the screen as to where, or how to buy one though. I ran to find my parents so I could tell them the good news. We had to act quickly.

"Mom, I found out how we can get enough money to pay for everything!" I said as I flew into the kitchen out of breath. My mother was angrily cutting an onion. She did not even look up at me she was so upset, so I yelled, "Ma! I found a money machine on television. Let's go to the store to see if we can buy one." She turned and asked, "How are we going to do this Bintell?"

"I just saw it. They have them on TV. This big machine was printing long sheets of money. It was spitting money out so fast, I could not see if they were $5 or $10 bills." She smiled lovingly. My father said nothing as he hurried to mail off the payment. She put down the knife, leaned over and kissed me on the forehead.

"Sweetheart that was a printing press you saw. Only the government is allowed to use those things to make money. If we use it, we will get in big trouble."

I was disappointed to say the least. But still, somewhere in the back of my mind, I was convinced a certain chosen few had the instructions on how to make their own homemade money machines, fully loaded, equipped with built in printing presses. If I could get my hands on those instructions, I would make my own money machine, hopefully just in time to save my family from financial ruin.

What would a homemade money machine's moving parts look like? Better yet, how many moving parts would it need to work for years without breaking down? If I could make a simple one, then everybody could have one, just like a toaster, or a stove. It would be like giving the entire world a money aspirin. There would be no more pain over money for anyone.

Like most people, I saw machines as intimidating, complicated things. From the cars my father fixed in his cold garage, to the insides of the toy train sets I got for Christmas, machines were complex things, with lots of confusing independent moving parts. Even still, machines fascinated me. Their precision, their reliability, the way they effortlessly did their job for years on end without ever the need to rest. Instead of a complex piece of equipment, what if money machines were as simple and easy to make as my favorite paper airplane?

Many days I would close my eyes and dream of being a money doctor so I could tell my parents, "Take two of these money aspirin and call me in the morning!" They belly-ached tirelessly about money. "Success is money my Boy" or, "Money is my best friend," were my father's battle cries. "Save your money and in time, your money will save you!" was my mother's mantra.

Mom told me stories over and over about my grandmother who had lived the second half of her life as a widow and how shrewd she was with money. When her daughters suggested she find a new husband, Grandma would say as she waived her hands to the heavens, "If I have my money, I do not need a new husband!"

I would sit and listen to them quietly, dying to ask the question, "Does anyone even know what money is made of?" but I never did. Just like my many days locked away in lab classes, I stayed quiet, afraid to ask the obvious, exposing what I did not know and embarrassing myself.

I figured that somewhere between all the talk from my parents about the value of hard work and me going to school to become an engineer, someone would tell me how to make a money machine, or the answer would become very obvious. I was wrong on both counts. Just like my classmates in a final exam, nobody said a word. I had to figure it out on my own.

WORK IS THE COLLECTION, CREATION & MAINTENANCE OF PRODUCTS FOR THE SOLE PURPOSE OF SALE TO PROFIT.

THE HUNT

ಜ

THE MOST SIGNIFICANT IMPROVEMENT TO THE WAY OF LIFE
FOR PEOPLE THROUGHOUT THE WORLD, WAS THE INDUSTRIAL
REVOLUTION & THE INVENTION OF THE MACHINE.

Although it should have been obvious that the people closest to me, with little or no money would not be able to tell me how to make a money machine, it was not. Being so young, I had no idea my parents and their friends were just as in the dark about money as I was.

In my naive eyes, they were making lots of money as they had homes and cars. Only now is it clear that these expensive things that kept them working so hard, yet hopelessly in debt, combined with their outlandish, at times ridiculous explanations about money, were the exact reason they were stuck in the "rat race" with no escape in sight.

"Money is the root of all evil!" was heard out of every adult mouth. This was very confusing, as these same people worked day in and day out for money to pay their mortgages, as if their lives depended on it.

When I asked my retired aunts and uncles about money, they would say, "Do not worry your head about money, my Son. If you do the right thing and work hard, money always comes." I had seen people in my own family work hard and die in poverty, so that response went in one ear, and right out the other.

There were ridiculous stories about aliens that made money for the government, or secret societies that kept track of how much money certain people were allowed to make in certain areas of the world. They almost convinced me there were secret numerical codes printed on the money itself and somehow linked to my social security number.

Some days I would grow impatient and ask the older men with candy and grocery stores in the neighborhood about money on my way to the park to play ball with friends. They would hold their heads, shaking them from side to side and say, "If I knew the answer to that question my Son, I would not be sitting here talking to you now. I would be on my yacht, or in my mansion." Others would say, "Money comes and goes young man. You are too young to worry about money. Enjoy your youth." But there was one man who sung a different tune altogether.

He looked just like the pictures of Superman's father in my comic books and he always had the cherry flavored icy I loved, so we became good friends. When I asked him how to make lots of money, he looked straight at me with his eyes ablaze and slowly leaned over the counter to give me some very valuable information. He said, "Son, if you really want to make money, you have got to be your own boss!"

That by far was the best answer I had ever gotten and I knew it as soon as it came out of his mouth. I took the valuable information, paid for the icy, shook my head yes and left the store. Even though the question as to how I would become my own boss was still a huge mystery, at least now I knew what direction to go in.

On my many summer jobs, I did my work quietly, waiting patiently for one of my many bosses to say anything I could use to build on the only piece of valuable information I had. Unfortunately, the messages I picked up were mostly arguments about getting to work on time and hourly rates of pay, which reminded me of the arguments over bills in my own home. Then an idea came to me. What if the answers were really on the money after all?

After cashing my checks, I would study the green slips of paper for money machine clues like I was being tested on it. There were confusing pictures with eyes embedded in pyramids, signatures and secret codes all over the crisp green pieces of paper. Maybe the money was made through a top secret partnership with the government and people whose main goal was to make money's design as confusing as possible? Other than the words, THE UNITED STATES OF AMERICA and, IN GOD WE TRUST, the information on the money itself made no sense to me at all.

MAN'S GREATEST WEAKNESS IS THAT HE/SHE WOULD RATHER BE ENTERTAINED, THAN INFORMED.

WHO HAS THE ANSWER?

❧

SUCCESS IS ABOUT STRATEGY AND PREPARATION. STRATEGY AND PREPARATION ARE ALL ABOUT INFORMATION.

This confusion over the ingredients needed to make money continued right up and through my college years. As graduation approached, the stories I heard of people making millions and billions of dollars on Wall Street made me certain that more than a few had beaten me to the punch by decoding the mystical green paper, and figured out how to make their money machines work.

With all the secret chatter about fraternities and private clubs, they must have had their money machine blueprints locked away in safe deposit boxes, or in their basements where only close friends could see. My suspicion made me ever so anxious to finish college as quickly as possible, and then get into the money game the first chance I got.

The money game was becoming a more dangerous one than I had bargained for. My mother's choice to use the family's life savings and send my sister and me to college caused an all out civil war in our home. My father insisted he and my mother split their life's savings in half the day after I left for my freshman year. I suppose he was deathly afraid of losing all his hard earned money on our education. Soon after I graduated, their divorce was finalized. Although my mother tried to tell us otherwise, I knew, at the heart of the conflict was my nemesis, money.

Looking back, my father was always resentful of the successful people he worked with, and for, who had information they'd purchased in college. He had not graduated from the 6th grade and I guess he felt his lack of college-bought information held him back from making his own money machine. Little did he know, in college, never once was a word about money uttered.

Instead, the professors hurled high speed formulas at me as if I were a catcher being pitched to in the major leagues. When I told my mother that never once had anyone mentioned the word money in any of my classes, she shrugged her shoulders and said, "I guess they are leaving those big money conversations up to your boss when you get your first big job." I skeptically resigned to the notion that all the glorious secrets of how to make a money machine would be revealed to me in a sacred ritual, on my first real job.

When the chance to play the money game finally came around, it was like standing still on the racetrack at the Indy 500. Everyone was secretively building themselves exotic money machines and flying past me at incredible speeds. Just like my classmates in all those lab classes, they kept their answers to themselves. This person was magically making a million a year. That person was making two million. Some were making hundreds of millions. Hedge fund managers were making billions.

Their money machines were sleek yellow and red sports cars with unlimited horsepower, just less the noisy engine. If they needed large sums of money for a yacht, or a new multi-million dollar home, they simply pressed the gas pedal of their money machine, the way I frequently hit the gas pedal driving in my mother's car on summer breaks.

In those first years in the money game, no matter how long and hard I worked, my money machine just would not spit out money as fast as theirs. Mine was always breaking down, as it was missing parts. To get the instruction on how to build a high speed money machine once and for all, I decided to make friends with the people who owned the fastest money machines in the land.

Just like the candy store owner had told me years ago, I chose to get close to the people who were always their own boss, no matter who they were working with or for. Maybe they would let me take theirs for a quick spin around the block.

"MONEY IS ONE OF THE MOST IMPORTANT SUBJECTS OF YOUR ENTIRE LIFE. SOME OF LIFE'S GREATEST ENJOYMENTS AND MOST OF LIFE'S GREATEST DISAPPOINTMENTS STEM FROM YOUR DECISIONS ABOUT MONEY. WHETHER YOU EXPERIENCE GREAT PEACE OF MIND OR CONSTANT ANXIETY WILL DEPEND ON GETTING YOUR FINANCES UNDER CONTROL."

- ROBERT G ALLEN — CEO, MICROSOFT

BIRTH OF A SALES ENGINEER

ಙ

SALESPEOPLE ARE MORE LIKELY TO BECOME CHIEF EXECUTIVE
OFFICERS AND PRESIDENTS OF A COMPANY THAN ALL OTHER
PROFESSIONALS COMBINED.

I made friends with the salespeople because they made more money than all other people on Earth. They showed me how their money machines worked, and I copied most everything about the way they put their machines together. The only thing is, I made mine just a little bit differently.

I did not just sell computer systems to top executives and presidents of companies like The Rockefeller Foundation, Conde Nast, Coca Cola, Duane Reade, Yahoo, and the National Hockey League, all the way down to the small mom and pop shops, I designed them as well. I was a Sales Engineer.

Meeting with one company at a time, I slowly realized that all companies, large, small and in between, were simple machines made with only three connected parts. No matter what the tag on the top of the machine read, they were all designed to spit out tons of money, and they all had only three parts inside.

The successful salespeople I would watch in amazement quietly making millions of dollars over my 20-year career were no

25

different than the companies I sold computer systems to. They themselves were key parts of their own money machine, made of the same three connected parts. The most powerful nations of the world worth trillions of dollars were just simple money machines made with those same three connected parts. Just like any company, their presidents were just like me, a salesman. I knew my money machine was working properly when people started saying, "Bintell is a machine."

From all my experiences as an engineer turned salesman, the most reliable machine I ever played with, was a formula.

SALESPEOPLE MAKE MORE MONEY THAN ALL OTHER PEOPLE ON EARTH.

TAKE IT FOR A SPIN

&

SUCCESS IS WHEN THE RAT RACE CHASES YOU.

Once I had my machine put together properly, it worked like a lucky charm. It practically turned itself on and began spinning around, spitting out money with each go-round. I watched it spin in amazement, thrilled I had finally gotten it to work. Then I hopped inside and sped around town for a while. I must admit, I wanted everyone to see me in it.

> "I did not want to repeat my parent's life. I saw in their lives a routine and a lack of dreaming, a lack of possibilities, a lack of passion. And I did not want to live without passion " Hugh Hefner- Creator of the Playboy Magazine Empire

Taking my joy ride through the city, I peeked into my rear view mirror and was surprised to see that success was frantically chasing after me. People flocked to me like seagulls flock to bread on the beach. By the time I got back home to park the money machine, I had so many people eagerly offering me opportunities for greater success, I could not keep track of them.

It was like a big secret I could not wait to let out. The best place to start would be in the schools. Give the money machines assembly instructions to the children first so they could get theirs built early in life. Once they were official money doctors, they would be unleashed on their parents to cure all their money aches and pains.

My wife was working as an assistant principal in an inner city high school that looked more like a pit stop for the penitentiary. I told her to take me to the worst classes in the school. The classes filled with gang members and kids feared by their teachers. If the machine could transform their lives, it would work on just about anyone.

The school was something out of an overdramatized horror movie about the inner city, only this was very real. There was a loud wave of noise you would hear at a concert or a boxing match as the fighters jump into the ring. Young girls were screaming at the top of their lungs and others were punching boys for the attention they probably were not getting at home. Pencils were flying and kids were standing on desks or running through the halls. Complete chaos. I walked through the halls in shock. Even though she'd told me the school was bad, I could not believe what I was seeing.

Even still, the kids were just like me in many ways. Confused by the drudgery of school, they felt it was not giving them what they really needed. They wanted the answers as to how to become popular and how to make a lot of money. Like most people at their age, popularity and how to make lots of money were the only things that could ever really get their attention and keep it.

They were watching their parents being abused by the rat race, overrun by bills and grumpy most of the time. Because their parents were fighting a losing battle, they had little hope that school would help them achieve success in their own lives. Lectures and speeches just would not cut it with this crowd. They needed results.

If you are sick, you need medicine. If you are being beaten up by a bully, you may need boxing or karate lessons. If a huge money machine is threatening to run you over, you need a steel caged pickup truck with huge air bags. These kids had nothing to protect them from a sure head on collision with a

$14 trillion machine called the United States rat race. They were like lambs being led to the slaughter.

Unlike a small group of wealthy children living in luxurious North Shore neighborhoods throughout the world, they had no money for new clothes for back to school, summer trips, ballet classes and other extracurricular activities. Some did not even have enough food to eat on a daily basis. Out of desperation, others were making poor choices to sell drugs, landing them in jail or worse, early graves. Some teens frustrated by the lack of success, were even taking their own lives. They needed real answers to real problems. I took a deep breath and started talking, choosing my words ever so carefully.

"THE CORPORATION IS THE 'MASTER', THE EMPLOYEE IS THE 'SERVANT.' BECAUSE THE CORPORATION OWNS THE MEANS OF PRODUCTION WITHOUT WHICH THE EMPLOYEE COULD NOT MAKE A LIVING, THE EMPLOYEE NEEDS THE CORPORATION MORE THAN VICE VERSA."

- PETER DRUCKER

THE BET

&

INFORMATION FROM THE PAST, COMPARED TO INFORMATION IN THE
PRESENT, HELPS YOU PREDICT THE FUTURE.

"**I** know you believe you have heard it all before. I know you think I am just another older man in a suit that really does not understand your aches and pains. You probably believe I have nothing to say that can help you, but I promise you, today you will receive something you can use to make your life better." They kept talking, ignoring me as if I was not even in the room, so I went for the jugular.

"I will make you a bet worth a few thousand dollars." They instantly got quiet. "If I do not teach you how the rich get rich, I will give someone in this room this $6,000 watch on my wrist. But if I do show you what money is really made of, you have to promise me you will use it to make yourself rich, no matter what!" A hush fell over the classroom and all eyes were instantly glued to mine.

"If I win this bet, you will only owe me a promise to choose success in whatever makes you happy…deal?" They all sat there silently looking at me with puppy dog eyes, so I took that as a yes. The bet was on.

"All people live two separate lives. One half of our life is social, and the other half is economic, financial or about money. Sometimes, no scratch that, all the time these two lives collide. Socio-economic status is a person's total value to the world. So if

30

you have a healthy social life and a healthy financial life then the world will see you as a complete success. Your social life cannot get too far without your financial life. They are connected and need each other to grow." Their eyes showed they were still interested, so I kept talking.

"People with a high socioeconomic status like musicians, athletes, and say, the President of the United States, are seen as very successful people. They are stars, superstars even, as millions of people love them, (their social life) and they are rich, (their economic life). For 91 percent of the people in the world, we chase after these two lives. But for the remaining nine percent of the people on Earth, a healthy social and economic life chases after them relentlessly. I am here to tell you exactly how to get these two lives to chase after you."

They sat there staring. Some rolled their eyes. One young man in the back asked the obvious question. "Are you successful?"

"That my young man is a great question to which the answer is, yes."

"So you are a millionaire?"

"No, not at this time." The entire class in unison let out a loud, "Ahhhhhhh!" I had to raise my hands and my voice as chaos almost broke out in the overcrowded classroom.

"In my life, I have made millions of dollars. Unfortunately, I made these millions for others. I have also socialized with very rich people. People you have all seen and admired on television. What these successful people had, I now have. What the companies I have made millions for had, I now have. They are rich because they were able to turn what I now have, into millions and even billions of dollars, as I am now in the process of doing. This incredibly valuable thing is exactly what I am here today to give to you." A young girl blurted out the obvious question.

"What is this thing?"

"This thing is a product. Specifically information." A

good amount of the kids wrinkled their brows in confusion.

"Information on how rich people turn your pain, into their money. I am willing to bet that if I give you this secret information, if you choose to, you will use it to make yourself rich." One young man said, "This guy is full of it." The teacher jumped in. "Class, why not let him finish? If he is not being straight with you, one of you will get his $6,000 watch. Remember?" I took off the watch and placed it on the desk in front of me and started talking again.

"You see, I know what causes you pain. For one, I know most people, young and old, would like to be loved and accepted by the world. It is a natural urge that makes us human. This is why 90 percent of you in this classroom are wearing Nikes sneakers. Nikes are for the in crowd. The popular people, right?" Nobody spoke.

"Nike is selling people colorful sneakers to protect them from the pain of social failure. Did you know that the owner of Nike started the company running from pain as he'd failed to become a star track and field athlete?"

A few kids responded, "No." with surprise written all over their faces.

"It is really nothing new. There are tons of companies doing the same thing, as they know the pain of being left out of the right social circle has been causing people deep emotional pain for generations. By the way most of the people in the halls were admiring each other's clothing as I walked to this classroom, it is obvious that many of you are running from this same pain. When I was your age, I ran from it as well. You see, you all trust that Nike sneakers will shield you from this pain, and this is why the owners of Nike are rich. The fact that those sneakers help you run fast and protect your feet from the hard concrete means very little in terms of their success. There are tons of other, cheaper sneakers that do just as good, or even better of a job, but still, you all choose Nike." The kid who said I was full of it sat back in his seat.

"More proof that being part of the in crowd is very important to many of you, is the large number of gangs that are popping up in this neighborhood. Believe it or not, gangs are very similar to some of the exclusive clubs for wealthy people I have managed to sneak into in my life. They use protection from the pain of social failure as bait to lure you in. The best gangs seek out the best and brightest of the world, as they can also provide you protection from the pain of financial failure. What if I could show you how to get the whole world to buy you like you were a Nike sneaker? What if everyone loved and desired your friendship without the risk and danger of being in a gang?" A young girl in the front of the class helped me out.

"That is true. You have to give him that. Most of you only join gangs to be popular. Some of you would not be so big and bad if you were not in a gang." Before anyone could respond to her, I jumped back in.

"Now let us talk money. I know that 91 percent of the seven billion people on Earth are in pain over the money they do not have. I know that salespeople are the richest people on the face of the Earth, as they turn things like Nike sneakers, cell phones, cars and computers into millions and billions of dollars. I also know that nine times out of 10, sneakers, cars, cell phones and computers are made by engineers."

"Okay, so how does that make YOU rich?" asked the same young man in the back of the class.

I smiled and said, "All companies are made of two parts. The part that engineers the product, and the part that sells that product. All other jobs besides the engineer and the salesman are there to make sure the engineer makes more products, and the salespeople sell more of those same products."

"Yes, and again, what does that have to do with you?"

"I am an electrical engineer." Again, there was silence. "I am also a salesman."

"So where does the social part come into all this?" asked a young girl after a brief pause.

"Because people only flock to things they feel are valuable, like a movie star or a shiny red sports car. What I am trying to say is, your social life is dependent on you turning yourself into something people will flock to. I am here to show you how to engineer a better you so you can sell yourself to the world. I am what you call a Sales-Engineer. I have designed a formula for social and financial success that I have used in my life to make others rich. It is like a treasure map to financial freedom. I like to think of this formula as a money machine. I am in the process of selling it to the world like a department store sells you a stove for your kitchen. You are the first people to see how it works. Soon, people all over the world will flock to it and both my social and economic lives will explode! I want to show you all the secrets of the rich. I want to show you how to make your very own money machine."

When I began explaining the three parts of the money machine and how easy it was to connect them, their eyes brightened and their ears perked up like puppies that had just smelled fresh food. The allure of social dominance and a money/ATM machine in their homes with an unlimited supply of money hypnotized them, as well as their teacher.

I knew I had power over them when the feared gang member sitting in the back of the class sweetly asked me, "When is that book coming out sir?" To this day, whenever he sees me, he tries to recite the three parts of the money machine I call, *The Formula.*

True to the genius of children, the uninterested class began making their own money machines from the experiences of their lives, confirming my suspicion that the youth are the innovators of tomorrow, while the elders are the keepers of tradition.

They dreamed up impressive new high speed money machines and identified the ways some of their favorite celebrities had made theirs. Ironically, the kids that had been written off as the worst students, came up with the most impressive money machines of the entire class.

After half an hour, I could see the light bulbs flickering in their eyes as I spoke. For at least a moment, they seemed hopeful. Like they suddenly had a tool they could use to control their lives for a change. They seemed to suddenly understand what role school played in designing their custom made money machine.

They began explaining how they themselves fit into the world economy as a machine and quickly caught on to the mechanics of the stock market when I explained it briefly. I left the school with my watch. Next, I set my sights on the adults.

I showed it to business owners, other engineers, doctors and finance people. They would say, "You are actually right. You might really be on to something here! Those are the keys to success. I never thought about making money and success that way before. And I do use this formula. We all do even though nobody calls it that. It is so simple, and obvious. Why did I not see this myself?"

The financial people called the three parts of the money machine instruments. They called the entire machine working together a vehicle, while the architects called it a model. The engineers called it an assembly. A couple that owned a restaurant called the three parts of *The Formula* ingredients. I put the ingredients together and called the machine, a formula.

I knew I had something special when one gentleman who owned an advertising company in New York said, "Okay, what do you want to do with this thing? Do you really want to help people, or do you just want to make a lot of money?"

Business owners said they knew exactly what they needed to do to make their business flourish with less work so they could have more time to spend with their families. They understood why certain business ventures in their past had failed, while others had prospered.

Those who were already successful said, "That is true. That is how I did it." Some said they could use it to become more powerful on their jobs, earning them that corner office they believed was out of their reach. Most importantly, they understood that a well-built money machine will run forever. I continued testing it for about five years on people from all walks of life with the intention of breaking it, but I could not, no matter how hard I tried. *The Formula* is my life's work and now, the time has come to let you take it for a spin. I am very anxious to see how fast you can make it go.

The remainder of this book has an instruction manual on how to assemble and use this money machine. It is also full of short stories of my life, broken into different acts, as the discovery of this money machine took place over my 40-year life. This book is designed to give you the only thing I would ever want from any financial book, a PhD in Success.

"FINANCIAL EDUCATION NEEDS TO BECOME A PART OF OUR NATIONAL CURRICULUM AND SCORING SYSTEMS SO THAT IT'S NOT JUST THE RICH KIDS THAT LEARN ABOUT MONEY... IT'S ALL OF US."

- DAVID BACH

ACT THREE

Success = Information + Commodities + Relationships = $$$

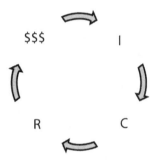

$$$ I

R C

OWNERS
MANUAL

ASSEMBLY INSTRUCTIONS INCLUDED

&

"THERE IS NO SUBSTITUTE FOR KNOWLEDGE. TO THIS DAY, I READ THREE NEWSPAPERS A DAY. IT IS IMPOSSIBLE TO READ A PAPER WITHOUT BEING EXPOSED TO IDEAS. AND IDEAS... MORE THAN MONEY... ARE THE REAL CURRENCY FOR SUCCESS."

- ELI BROAD - BUSINESS LEADER AND PHILANTHROPIST

The Formula works like a spinning wheel, or better yet, an engine. It is what many call organic. Meaning, it feeds off of itself and grows bigger and bigger each time it spins. You have mastered its use when you have a bank account full of money and are the proud owner a new hot commodity each time it spins around in your life.

When your money machine is working, if you do not pay attention, you will miss it, as its behavior can be as fast and as silent as electricity running through a wire. If it turns on and then turns off because it is not put together properly, you will not even know it was there. The goal of this section is to show you exactly how to assemble your machine so it does not turn off while you are using it.

There are illustrations to follow that show exactly how *The Formula* spins and behaves so you can be ready and watch as your success is happening, each and every step of the way. Let's take a look at exactly how this money machine works.

SUCCESS IS SOMETHING THAT TURNS OUT AS PLANNED

HOW THE MACHINE BEHAVES

❧

A FORMULA IS THE ONLY MACHINE ON EARTH THAT WILL NEVER STOP WORKING.

This formula / money machine has three parts and produces social and financial success in three simple steps. The first piece of *The Formula* is where the information identifies, creates and ultimately sells the second piece of *The Formula* which is the commodity. Then, the commodity attracts the third piece of *The Formula* which are the relationships, who will buy the commodity and make it so hot, you'll end up with tons of money in your pocket.

At that final step, the relationships in addition to money, will provide more information called feedback, so your money machine keeps going around and around, making more money and spitting out more exciting new hot commodities forever and ever.

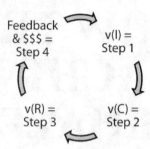

Here is a recap of the way *The Formula* behaves, one step at a time.

1. Information identifies, creates and then sells the commodity(s) as **Step 1**, which moves us to **Step 2**.
2. Then, the commodities at **Step 2**, attracts relationships to move *The Formula* to **Step 3**.
3. Next, at **Step 3**, the relationships produce money as well as more information called feedback to get us to **Step 4**.
4. Then, this feedback from relationships at **Step 4**, added to the information you will continue to pump inside the money machine on your own at **Step 1**, keeps *The Formula* spinning and producing success and money forever.

People like Martha Stewart who's first commodity was a cookbook, or Ralph Lauren who's first commodity was a necktie, in time, using *The Formula*, created so many hot commodities, they now have mega successful lifestyle brands. They own and sell commodities for every type of pain you could encounter in a lifetime, which has produced billions for each of them.

The best part about the way *The Formula* works is, once you have it working for you, unlike all the other people of the world who chase after success, stuck inside the rat race, success will hunt you down and offer you all you could ever want and more. You just have to be ready for it when it happens because when it does, the only way to get it to stop, is to stop paying attention to the information from **Step 4**, or stop feeding it information at **Step 1**. Otherwise, success will hunt for you relentlessly. Successful blockbuster actors like George Clooney receive hundreds of offers for movies each and every day without fail. He picks one.

Pushing information in and out of this money machine is like turning the ignition key in a car on and off. Information is the heart and soul of this money machine. Because of information's extreme value to success, we can leave nothing about how information creates success, financial or social unclear. So, let's identify the three ways your money machine will use information to "make money." I call them, the Information Commandments.

THE MAJORITY OF THE INFORMATION WE RECEIVE TO HELP US REACH SUCCESS COMES FROM OUR ENVIRONMENT. IF YOU HAVE NO VALUABLE INFORMATION, CHANGING YOUR ENVIRONMENT IS STEP ONE.

UNDER THE HOOD

ॐ

This Money Machine is made with three parts.

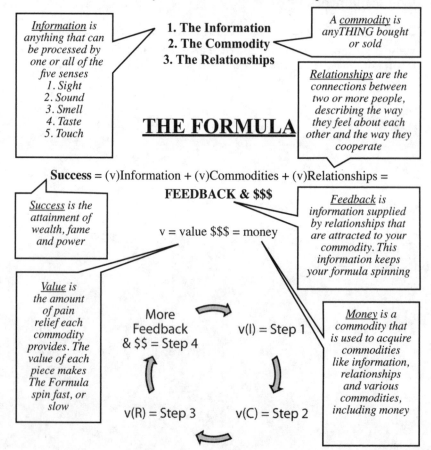

Information is anything that can be processed by one or all of the five senses
1. Sight
2. Sound
3. Smell
4. Taste
5. Touch

1. The Information
2. The Commodity
3. The Relationships

A *commodity* is anyTHING bought or sold

Relationships are the connections between two or more people, describing the way they feel about each other and the way they cooperate

THE FORMULA

Success = (v)Information + (v)Commodities + (v)Relationships =
FEEDBACK & $$$

Success is the attainment of wealth, fame and power

v = value $$$ = money

Feedback is information supplied by relationships that are attracted to your commodity. This information keeps your formula spinning

Value is the amount of pain relief each commodity provides. The value of each piece makes The Formula spin fast, or slow

More Feedback & $$ = Step 4

v(I) = Step 1

v(R) = Step 3   v(C) = Step 2

Money is a commodity that is used to acquire commodities like information, relationships and various commodities, including money

44

INFORMATION COMMANDMENTS

❧

"GROWING UP, MY FRIENDS AND I COULDN'T UNDERSTAND WHY PEOPLE COULDN'T SEE THINGS THE WAY WE DID. WE DIDN'T UNDERSTAND WHY THEY DIDN'T SEE VALUE IN WHAT WE DID."

- BILL GATES

Information is the most powerful commodity on Earth. The human brain processes 40 billion bits of information each second. Using information is the only way you can insert instructions in the human brain without the pain of an operation. The good news is, information is an equal opportunity employer of success. It is free to the entire world.

Here are three Information Commandments that will keep your money machine running in high gear, or cause it to seize and stop producing money for you completely.

The three commandments are:

1. Information discovers/identifies a commodity's ability to relieve pain.
2. Information creates a commodity.
3. Information sells a commodity.

Now, let's see exactly how they behave in action.

COMMANDMENT
I

&

COMMANDMENT I:
INFORMATION IDENTIFIES PAIN RELIEF IN A COMMODITY

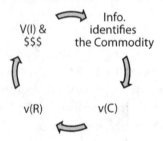

The golden rule of information and discovery is, wherever there is pain, there is a need for a product / commodity to cure it. One third of your ability to engineer success for yourself will come from your ability to simply recognize the pain of the world.

Christian Audigier saw a trend in tattoos and realized there were millions of people who did not want to go through the physical pain of actually tattooing their bodies. So, he put tattoos on tee-shirts and in no time at all, he was worth half a billion dollars with a lifestyle brand that has tattoos on everything from tee-shirts, to hats, to jackets. He calls this lifestyle brand, Ed Hardy.

As the number of millionaires and billionaires continues to explode all over the world, there are many people like Mr. Christian Audigier that have made a choice to recognize value in commodities, while others choose only to see value in a commodity when they need to relieve some personal pain they are in.

The famous Taxi Cab Billionaire is a prime example of a person who can recognize pain relief in a product for the purpose of profit, as opposed to recognizing pain relief only for the purpose of using it.

Tamir Sapir, the famous Taxi Cab Billionaire started off driving a cab in New York City in the late 1970s. When he was finished picking and choosing which commodities he would buy and sell for profit 30 years later, he was worth close to $2 billion.

After driving a cab for a few years, he purchased an electronics store in Manhattan. From there, he chose to buy and sell oil and fertilizer stock as people always need oil to protect them from the pain of the cold, and they always need food to protect them from the pain of hunger.

A few years of success with oil and fertilizer stocks, the feedback he received from friends and customers led him to purchase real estate. By the time it was over, and he finally sold his real estate, he had a reputation for success known throughout the world as the Taxi Cab Billionaire.

That story is cute, but if you are still not convinced that simply recognizing pain can make you wildly successful, I guess there is no better example of a person who can recognize value in a commodity, than the grand master himself, who up until the Great Recession of 2008, held the title as the second richest man on Earth.

When you talk about success by way of picking and choosing commodities, this man needs no introduction. When you talk about success chasing someone and the Law of Attraction, you have to talk about Warren Buffett.

Mr. Buffett has developed a cult following for his ability to recognize value in companies that other people see as worthless. Just the rumor of Mr. Buffett purchasing stock in a company can send its value soaring, as people instantly start asking themselves, "What did we miss? What does he see in this company? He must know something we do not. Let us buy some too." In 2008, Warren Buffett purchased a piece of a company called BYD increasing the company's value five times and earning its founder Wang Chuanfu, an additional $4 billion.

Success chases him no matter where he goes. Every year, Mr. Buffett holds a retreat where investors, young and old, hoping to get a chance to do business with him, or at the very least, have his ability to recognize value rub off on them, come from far and wide to steal as much information as they can. This yearly retreat personifies the true meaning of The Law of Attraction and proof that once you have your machine built properly, success will chase after you no matter where you go.

Success = (Recognize Value) + (Any Commodity) + (The World) = **Law of Attraction**

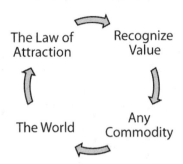

The Law of Attraction

Recognize Value

The World

Any Commodity

A very simple man at heart, Mr. Buffett has been quoted as saying, "I try not to get involved with any company that I do not understand." Ironically his best friend is Bill Gates. Mr. Gates who up until the Great Recession of 2008-2009 was the richest man on earth, proving that valuable commodities attract other valuable commodities, even if they happen to be people.

Even though Mr. Buffet has for many years enjoyed being one of the richest men on Earth, he has newcomers nipping at his heels. Recognizing value in commodities can not only make you a billionaire, it can actually make you recession proof. Mr. John Paulson, a relative newcomer to the Billionaire Boys Club is proof of that.

In my short 20-year stint in the rat race, I have been subject to two recessions. Both the recession of the late 1990s and the Great Recession of late 2008-2009, were due to people overvaluing one commodity and driving its price up so far, it broke the money machine of the United States and the world. In the late 1990s it was the value of Internet companies. In the Great Recession of 2008-2009, it is the value of real estate.

People like Mr. John Paulson recognized that the value of real estate was just too high. He was able to sidestep a recession that bankrupted thousands of others, turning him into a billionaire. When all the smoke caused by the explosion of this $14 trillion money machine called the United States of

America cleared, Mr. Paulson emerged with his money machine more than intact.

Mr. Paulson is a former hedge fund manager, which is a fancy title for people with so many formulas and behavioral models up their sleeve, they are sure to make more money than 99 percent of the people on Earth. Mr. Paulson knew that if people continued to use their homes as their personal ATM machines, essentially abusing one commodity inside the money machine, it would break down. When this happened, the value of all the other commodities in the machine would fall along with it. When a national money machine behaves this way, it is called a market crash.

So, Mr. Paulson bet that the value of real estate would go down instead of going up. In the world of finance, this success formula for making money is called "shorting the market." Placing this bet by using his ability to recognize value in a commodity made all the difference in the world.

While the breakdown of the US economy sent millions without a formula like Mr. Paulson's to the unemployment line, or worse, bankruptcy, Mr. Paulson's personal money machine quietly gave him $14 billion without so much as a stutter.

Success = (Recognize Unrealistic Value) + (Real Estate) + (Stock Market) = **$14 billion**

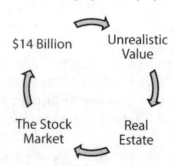

$14 Billion   Unrealistic Value

The Stock Market   Real Estate

Now, it should be clear that recognizing value is critical to keeping your success formula working smoothly. Okay, so you have recognized value in something. You realize it relieves pain and people will trade money to have it. Cool. Lay up job.

But what if there are no valuable commodities just lying around? What if there are no "natural resources" just waiting for you to come along and get rich selling them? Are you just going to accept failure? Or are you going to make something from nothing? Well, inventing, and re-inventing is a simple, easy, and neat little trick made from four magic words.

ALTHOUGH MOST PEOPLE ARE INSTANTLY BORED BY THE WORD, INFORMATION IS THE MOST POWERFUL COMMODITY ON EARTH. IT CAN TURN RAGS TO RICHES AS WELL AS TURN A HUMAN BEING INTO A TOOL AS USEFUL AS A WRENCH OR A PENCIL.

INFORMATION IS WHAT CREATES HOT COMMODITIES!

COMMANDMENT II

❦

"THE LIFEBLOOD OF OUR BUSINESS IS THE MONEY WE SPEND ON RESEARCH & DEVELOPMENT. WE HAVE TO CONTINUOUSLY CREATE NEW INNOVATION THAT LETS PEOPLE DO SOMETHING THEY DID NOT THINK THEY COULD DO THE DAY BEFORE."

— STEVE BALLMER

COMMANDMENT II:
INFORMATION CREATES THE COMMODITY

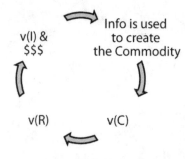

Info is used to create the Commodity

v(I) & $$$

v(R)   v(C)

> "Early on in my career I realized my job was not just to give people clothes they wanted, but it was to also give it to them in a way they did not know they wanted it"
> Kenneth Cole

O nce successful people have recognized pain in life, if there is not one already available, they instantly focus on creating a product to cure it. If there is one already available, they re-invent it and make it better.

These people do not wait around for anyone to tell them

SUCCESS = I + C + R

they are not an engineer and they are not smart enough to create. They choose success and grab it by providing the world with pain relief. In America, the idea is all you need. The ownership of the idea as a product is called "Intellectual Property" and the government will help you protect and own it with a patent.

The process to create anything is always the same. Instead of doing it the painful way, what if we did it the painless way? This question; this desire to ask ourselves, "What if there is a better way?" is the basis of growth, advancement, better known as evolution.

THE MOTHER OF ALL CREATION

Instead of doing it the painful way, *What if* we tried it the painless way?

> *"We must continually reinvent ourselves, responding to changing times with innovative new business models "* Akira Mori – President & Chief Executive of the Mori Trust

The creators of Google said, "*Instead of* finding information on the web by tracking the number of times a website has been visited, *what if* we used the number of relationships one site has with other sites to find information on the Internet?" The creators of Google are today worth billions.

Lonnie G. Johnson was an engineer for NASA who one day while experimenting in his bathroom watched as a burst of water so strong rifled past his face, it sent strong shock waves through the bathroom. Mr. Johnson recognized value in the unusual occurrence and asked himself, "*Instead of* using air pressure to launch things into space, *what if* we used air pressure to make a really cool water gun?" With that question, the Super Soaker water gun hit the general public earning $1 billion in total sales to date. Forget pain relief, this hot commodity has created pleasure packed summer days for children around the world, making Lonnie Johnson a very successful individual.

But there is nobody more famous for mastering this process of creation than the most famous creator of them all,

53

Mr. Benjamin Franklin. When you consider that commodities become money when people buy them, it is no surprise that his face appears on the $100 bill.

Benjamin Franklin had very bad eyesight. Without his glasses, he could barely read. He had glasses for short distances and another pair for long distances. Taking them off and on all the time became a drain on his time and energy so, Benjamin decided to make a change.

He said, "*Instead of* taking these two glasses on and off all day, *what if* I had one half of the lens for long distances and the other half for short?" With this question, the bifocal lens was created.

Mr. Franklin did not stop asking himself this life changing question there. He asked the same question about four times that we know of. His brother was in serious physical pain so he created the first flexible urinary catheter. He created the lightning rod to protect homes and ships from lightning strikes, the iron furnace which was an improvement to the wooden fireplace which led him to establish the first fire company and the first fire insurance company in order to help people live safely.

He made improvements to ship hulls to protect them from flooding in battle. He created the odometer to keep track of his distances as a postmaster and in his old age, he created the wooden arm so he could grab books from the top shelf of his library that were out of reach.

George Washington Carver must have been in the same classes as Benjamin Franklin. He invented 300 ways to use the peanut. He went on to use peanuts to create makeup, linoleum, shaving cream, paper, metal polish, bleach, buttermilk, ink, cosmetics, gasoline, dyes, plastics, paint and nitroglycerin.

Albert Einstein created the famed Theory of Relativity which has to be the most famous formula of all. Although he did not participate in its actual creation, $E=mc2$ laid the foundation for the creation of the atomic bomb, proving that a formula has universal application.

Miles Davis is known as the only musician to change the face of modern music five times. He invented The Cool, Funk, Modal Jazz and Jazz Fusion. The story goes that Miles was always jealous of the great creator of Bebop Jazz music, Mr. Dizzy Gillespie.

Dizzy's ability to play his trumpet at incredibly high speeds was envied by the world, as well as Miles Davis. Try as he might, Miles just could not play as fast as Dizzy. So, he said, "*Instead of* playing fast, *what if* I played really, really slow?" With that, a new style of music was born called, The Cool. He continued to behave this way, developing a reputation for creating and more importantly, creating again. To his credit, he is the best selling Jazz musician in history. While other Jazz artist had to leave the United States to find limited success abroad, Miles enjoyed pop star status at home, making him the richest Jazz artist of his time.

Now, the question is, how did he and other creators like him, turn their inventions into so much money?

"EVERY PROBLEM IS AN OPPORTUNITY IN DISGUISE."
- BENJAMIN FRANKLIN, INVENTOR OF THE BI-FOCAL LENS.

COMMANDMENT III

ॐ

"NO MATTER WHAT YOUR PRODUCT IS, YOU ARE ULTIMATELY IN THE EDUCATION BUSINESS. YOUR CUSTOMER NEEDS TO BE CONSTANTLY EDUCATED ABOUT THE MANY ADVANTAGES OF DOING BUSINESS WITH YOU, TRAINED TO USE YOUR PRODUCT MORE EFFECTIVELY, AND TAUGHT HOW TO MAKE NEVER-ENDING IMPROVEMENT IN THEIR LIVES."
— ROBERT G ALLEN

COMMANDMENT III:
INFORMATION TURNS COMMODITIES INTO MONEY

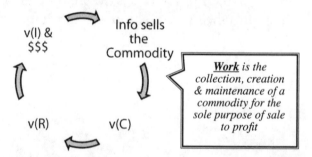

Info sells the Commodity

v(I) & $$$

v(R)

v(C)

Work is the collection, creation & maintenance of a commodity for the sole purpose of sale to profit

Rule number one in making money is, people only buy things they trust will cure their pain. So selling anything is simply a matter of selling trust in its pain relief. The product you are selling really has nothing to do with your success. If you want people to buy ANY product and turn it into a hot commodity, you have got to get them to trust in its ability to relieve pain. Luckily, the tools of the trust trade are the three individual parts of this money machine called *The Formula*.

TRUST = SALE

THE CREED OF TRUST STATES...

If you deliver the right information, own or can create the most valuable of commodities, and surround yourself with the right relationships, people will trust you and ANYTHING you are selling.

People will study the tragic story of Bernie Madoff and his abuse of trust to make money for hundreds of years to come. Bernie Madoff will live on as the all time number one abuser of trust as the creator of the largest "PONZI" scheme (a money machine with no commodity inside) in the history of the United States worth $50+ billion.

Mr. Madoff learned how to build an imaginary money machine first as a stock broker, then as an investment advisor and then as chairman of the NASDAQ. The significance of his impressive resume is simple. Most people use their resume as information to gain the trust of employers to get a job. Mr. Madoff on the other hand used his resume as information to gain the trust of thousands of investors so they would give him all of their money.

Mr. Madoff told his customers he was going to use their money to buy and sell high value commodities for steady profit. In reality, he was taking the money he received from one investor, to pay another. Mr. Madoff's elaborate money machine had not a single commodity inside it. Well, maybe it had one; being him disguising himself as a trustworthy investment advisor by way of his squeaky clean image.

If anyone was qualified to pull this type of operation off, it is a chairman of the NASDAQ. With such a trustworthy title under his belt, along with trusted relationships with every financial professional on Earth, Mr. Madoff seduced actors, athletes, other investment companies, as well as hard working people across the globe who begged him to manage their life's savings.

Success = (Résumé) + (Money Formulas & Mr. Madoff) + (Powerful Relationships) = **$51 Billion**

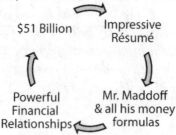

$51 Billion — Impressive Résumé — Mr. Maddoff & all his money formulas — Powerful Financial Relationships

Even after the FCC, an agency with the sole purpose of monitoring fraud in the stock market was told Mr. Madoff was running a money machine without a single commodity except his image inside it, he was so trustworthy in the eyes of the entire investment world, he was untouchable. If not for the Great Recession of 2009, where people were pulling their money out of the stock market in fear of a market crash, Mr. Madoff's imaginary money machine would never have been exposed.

Failure = Résumé + Only Mr. Madoff's Image + Unsuspecting Investors = **-$0.00**

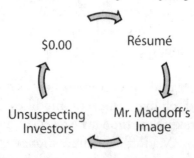

$0.00 — Résumé — Mr. Maddoff's Image — Unsuspecting Investors

So, every single piece of information (SALES PITCH) regarding the value of your commodity should be designed with the intention of gaining the trust of those that will buy it. No trust, no sale.

Although a creative mixture of *The Formula* is often used to turn products into hot commodities and unlimited money, other than your own behavior, one of the best ways to get people to believe your commodity is worthy of their trust, is to get other people and/or things that are already trusted, to speak on its behalf. Trusted role models can sell just about anything, to just about anyone.

Relationships, valuable and strategic ones, can sell enough of your products to people and in places beyond your reach, saving you time and energy, making you very, very successful in the process. Successful people know they will ultimately be judged by the company they keep. They know the business of making money is ALL about relationships.

Clothing designers who are selling more of a dream and a lifestyle than actual clothes to protect people from the painful elements of the world use trusted celebrities to sell their clothing for them.

Louis Vuitton, better known as LVMH, the multi-billion dollar luxury clothing empire owned by billionaire Arnold Renault, uses trusted artist and movie stars like Madonna and Scarlet Johansen to sell their scarves, handbags and sunglasses to the lifestyle obsessed public looking for pain relief from the worst emotional pain of them all; mediocrity.

Zhou Chengjian turned himself into the $2.6 billion man by doing pretty much the same thing in China. This business model of endorsing products with trusted human beings has and continues to turn commodities into millions and billions of dollars for one reason; people model every aspect of their lives after models for success.

"IN THE 1960S, IF YOU INTRODUCED A NEW PRODUCT TO AMERICA, 90% OF THE PEOPLE WHO VIEWED IT FOR THE FIRST TIME BELIEVED IN THE CORPORATE PROMISE. THEN 40 YEARS LATER IF PERFORMED THE SAME EXERCISE, LESS THAN 10% BELIEVED IT WAS TRUE. THE FRACTURING OF TRUST IS BASED ON THE FACT THAT THE CONSUMER HAS BEEN LET DOWN."

- HOWARD SCHULTZ - CEO & FOUNDER OF STARBUCKS COFFEE.

THE COMMODITY

৪৩

INFORMATION, COMMODITIES, RELATIONSHIPS, MONEY & SUCCESS
ARE ALL COMMODITIES TO BE BOUGHT AND SOLD.

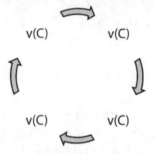

v(C) v(C)

v(C) v(C)

O nce you use information to identify or create your valuable commodity, your money machine will be in second gear and ready to turn your commodity into social and financial success. The amount of pain your commodity cures and how trustworthy you both are will dictate how much success it will provide. To help with the process, the commodity as part of your success / money machine does two things.

- **RELIEVES PAIN**
- **ATTRACTS RELATIONSHIPS**

Commodities like a cherry red sports car or an even better example, music, send out their own information that can sell them without much help. In a perfect world, this information will cause people to come running to buy it.

Unfortunately, this is not a perfect world, so owners of commodities use additional information to avoid the risk of their success / money machines breaking down on them. Remember, you are a part of your money machine as the most important trustworthy product people will buy, along with the product you create or identify of course. If you and your product are valuable and trustworthy, both of you will soon become so hot, you will be on fire.

Success = I + [You + Commodity + Info] + R = **$$$**

$$$ I

R   You
           C+I

In light of how important it is to your success for people to buy you, before we do anything, let's make sure we know exactly how to turn ourselves into a hot commodity because, if people do not trust in us, they will never buy our commodity, no matter how much pain it relieves.

People who are seen as valuable can sell their time for millions, as well as tons of their commodities in a package deal to millions of people throughout the world. An example of a person who has successfully "commoditized" herself would be a singer like Madonna, who can sell her time singing in a concert for millions in just one night. She can also sell her songs and talent to perform in movies sold in a CD or a DVD, or on television.

People trapped in the rat race, who are usually not seen as valuable commodities as they are easily replaced, are left with no other money making options but to sell their time for minimum wages.

After we understand how to turn ourselves into a commodity, we will take a quick look at the four types of pain people encounter in life so you understand why a certain commodity is valuable, and why another one is not. This way, you can begin to think about what types of pain relieving commodities you will create and why people should buy them. It is important to remember, the most valuable commodities can cure all four types of human pain, while others can cure only one.

WAYS TO TURN YOURSELF INTO A VALUABLE COMMODITY

- Develop a reputation for success.
- Inform the public about the pain you relieve.
- Collect large amounts of information on ways to identify, create and sell one or more valuable commodity(s).
- Develop and display extreme talent in one or more commodities or areas of expertise.
- Create and/or sell large amounts of valuable commodities.
- Adorn, and surround yourself with large amounts of valuable commodities, human or non-human.
- Collect large amounts of valuable relationships that are ready, willing and able to share their information, commodities and relationships with you.
- All of the above.

Now, let's make sure we understand how to be a creator of a commodity, instead of just a consumer. When most of us are in pain, we understand exactly what we need to buy to make that pain go away. But if we were suddenly challenged to create a commodity that people would buy, most people would be lost. Successful people know exactly why you buy one type of pain relief as opposed to another. With this information, they can easily create a product that you will see as valuable enough to buy. Now, so will you.

The people of the world that work for money to relieve themselves from life's four aches and pains call their work, "The Cost of Living." The people who create products to profit from the worlds need to relieve itself from pain call their work, "Commerce."

Products that keep the national and international money machines spinning fast enough to become hot commodities become that way because they relieve one, or all of the four types of pain for humanity. The four types of pains are listed below.

THE (4) TYPES OF PAIN

Physical Pain	Emotional Pain
Loss of Energy	Loss of Time

EXAMPLES OF PAIN RELIEF

1. Physical pain is cured by medicine, doctors, clothing and homes that protect us from the elements.
2. Emotional pain like loneliness and heartbreak is cured by commodities like music, entertainment, a therapist, and love.
3. Losses of energy are cured by commodities like cars and computers that help us reach our goals quickly, with little energy spent. This type of pain relief is called efficiency.
4. Losses in time are usually cured by the same commodities that cure a loss of energy.

(NOTE: Some pains can cause others. Example: If you are in physical pain, it can lead to emotional pain.)

Even if people trust your commodity enough to buy it,

it is unlikely that you will be able to sell enough of it on your own to turn it into millions and billions of dollars. Unless a single one of your commodities is sold for millions, there is just not enough time in the day for you to come in contact with that many people by yourself. This is where relationships turn your money machine into a "turbo charged vehicle."

The best way to save yourself the time and energy of turning your commodity into millions is to use relationships. The right relationships make the business of turning your commodity into a hot one all across the globe quick and easy. Why? Because, they can sell your commodity in places and at times you never could on your own.

SALES IS THE DELIVERY OF INFORMATION TO SELL A COMMODITY TO ONE PERSON.

MARKETING IS THE DELIVERY OF INFORMATION TO SELL A COMMODITY TO MILLIONS OF PEOPLE.

THE RELATIONSHIP

ॐ

EVERY RELATIONSHIP YOU WILL EVER HAVE IS THE RESULT OF SOME COMMODITY OF VALUE YOU POSSESS. BUSINESS IS ALL RELATIONSHIPS.

This is the fun part. Friends and relationships make us feel good about ourselves and for good reason. Their advantage in business is, relationships as part of the money machine sell lots of your commodities for you, but they also do something else just as important. In addition to keeping *The Formula* spinning around and around, they also do this:

1. Customer relationships purchase the commodity turning it into money.
2. Sales, marketing and partner relationships send out information of your commodities pain relief, helping to sell lots of it at times and in places you never could.
3. Manufacturing relationships can actually make millions of units of your product inexpensively, so you can sell them and make large profits. They will also provide you with information on the best ways to create your next commodity.
4. All of the above relationships provide valuable information on ways to create, sell, and identify more valuable commodities. This information is called feedback. When mega-successful companies or worldwide celebrities and

pop stars stop listening to this feedback, their days of success are numbered as feedback keeps *The Formula* spinning forever.

Success = Information + Commodities + Relationships = **$$$ + Feedback**

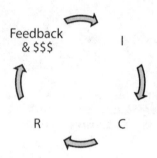

Feedback
& $$$
I
R   C

Anna Sui, the mother of vintage clothing design, made her world debut in 1991, right in the middle of the two titans of fashion, Versace and Chanel in their era of dominance. With support from relationships with super-model friends like Naomi Campbell and Linda Evangelista wearing her clothes in Paris, as well as walking in her first fashion show, she became an instant success and force to be reckoned with in the ultra competitive world of high fashion.

She instantly began receiving orders from around the world for her clothes. Soon, an associate convinced her to open a boutique in New York's Soho District. She has been an icon in fashion ever since.

The rest of this book shows how I found this success/ money machine I call *The Formula* one night when I least expected it. The book presents itself in a compilation of short stories. The stories overlap because I did not find the pathways to this money machines design one after the other. Many times, I had to go back into my past to find clues, and then connect them to things I discovered later.

Once you can use *The Formula* in any situation, you have mastered its use. Now, success is in a box and it has a name. If you continue reading this book and get into the simple machine you will find inside, it is guaranteed to take you on nothing short of the ride of your life! My hope is that you will use this machine to bring you all the money and success you have ever dreamed possible.

Don't hesitate to highlight key points throughout the book as you read it. I have provided a workbook as the final chapter so you can practice making your own money machines from scratch.

Most importantly, you will soon see that you have always had this formula. You are just as I was, caught so deep inside the rat race, running after success so fast, you were running right past it.

WHAT SEPARATES US FROM ANIMALS, MAKING US HUMAN ON THE MOST BASIC OF LEVELS, IS OUR ABILITY TO COOPERATE & SUCCESSFULLY WORK TOGETHER.

Warm Regards,

Bintell Powell

Creator of...The Formula...

ACT FOUR

Success = Information + Commodities + Relationships = $$$

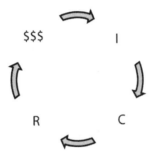

THE RAT RACE

THE FORMULA'S BIRTH

❧

1% OF THE POPULATION CONTROLS MORE THAN 50% OF ITS WEALTH.

> 73% of all US businesses are mom and pop shops or what business people call, sole proprietors

Growing up on the edge of the wealthy North Shore of Long Island New York was just like watching an episode of The Lifestyles of The Rich & Famous through a cloudy, cobwebbed basement window. After years of instability, moving from one place to the next in search of a comfortable place to call home, my parents finally saved enough money to purchase their lifelong dream of a very modest home, just across the main road from the incredible Estates of Old Westbury, Sands Point, Manhasset, Brookville and Muttontown in Long Island, New York.

These neighborhoods were filled with architects, engineers, movie and music producers, doctors, bankers, professional athletes, lawyers, presidents and vice presidents of many large worldwide companies, but most of the people in these neighborhoods, were successful small business owners.

My father was very proud of himself. As the breadwinner of our family, this hard working auto mechanic, who never made it past the 6th grade felt he had achieved the American Dream. In his eyes, he was an absolute success.

On the surface, we seemed like any successful American family. But unlike the wealthy people across the road, life for us was a constant struggle to pay the heating bill, the light bill, and the mortgage. We lived our life in constant fear that we may lose everything, if my father lost his job.

There were often arguments and bickering between my parents around our basic needs and how they would find money to pay for them. At times, it was like being trapped in a bad dream and not being able to wake up.

Although I had an idea from television shows that there were some people who enjoyed the extreme comforts of a life equipped with mansions, yachts, limousines, and dinner parties alongside Olympic-sized swimming pools, it was not until after we moved from the South Shore of Long Island, to the North Shore, that I got a chance to see the difference between the two ways of life, up close and personal.

On those special occasions when my parents splurged and took my sister and me to one of the many expensive restaurants in the area, I would sit and listen quietly to the well dressed businessmen with their families, as they talked about the business contacts they shared at work.

They would say things like, "I have a guy who can get my shipments through customs in two days for 30 percent less than most, and he will even do drops and pick-ups at most locations for no extra charge." Those statements were usually followed by, "Yeah, my guy can do that for me as well, and he charges me once every three months. Our kids go to the same summer camp, so he takes care of my packages before everyone else's."

Although we lived check-to-check and in the shadows of these complex and successful people, I always felt that if they lived and breathed the same air as me, there was a chance that in

Small companies produce 13 times more ideas for products than those of large multi -billion dollar corporations

time, I could achieve their confident, matter of fact posture towards success. I was convinced there had to be a blueprint, or some formula for success the people on the south side of town just did not have. I knew that if I kept my eyes and ears open, one day, I was going to get my hands on that blueprint and then, I would share it with the world.

Hoping to arm me with a profession she felt would pay off in the long run, my mother demanded I pursue a degree in electrical engineering at the ripe old age of nine. Although I wanted to go to school for something exciting, like international business, by the time I was in junior high school, I relinquished to her strong recommendation because, from what I saw on television, engineers made things like boats, bridges and airplanes.

If I could learn to make planes and boats, maybe I could start my own company just like the successful people I was obsessed with across the road. Then I would be just like my old friend from the candy store who had advised me years earlier. As it turns out, I got my chance to be the international businessman, as well as the engineer my mother wanted me to be, all at the same time.

When I finally graduated, the country was in a full-fledged recession. The older college graduates who had been out for a whole year scared me to death when they told me, "You do not want to get out here. If you are smart, you will stay in school. When you get out here, there won't be any jobs for you." How was I going to explain this to my mother? I was terrified of what was waiting for me.

When that high paying job did not magically appear, my father chastised my mother and said, "You paid all this money to give this kid a top-notch education and he can't even get a job!" I was so ashamed I had not landed my dream job designing submarines or airplanes for some big engineering firm, I could not even look my parents in their eyes.

To make matters worse, every hiring manager I

interviewed with asked me the same question. "Your resume says you are an engineer. Why do you want to be in sales?" But little did my parents, the hiring managers and I know, this stumbling block that I saw as the end of my life, turned out to be a blessing, and the birth of *The Formula*.

Engineering jobs were nonexistent for a young engineer with no experience in the recession of the early 1990s, so all my dreams of a high paying job and a bright future were shattered. Buying that big home and that shiny BMW were out of reach for me. To make matters worse, I was in desperate need of money to pay student loans and help my mother survive the financial upheaval of her nasty divorce. When I looked through the New York Times classified section, the highest paying jobs were for salespeople.

While the entry level salaries for engineers were listed at $35,000 a year, the entry level jobs for salespeople were double, many times triple that. Luckily, I had done some telemarketing sales for extra money before graduation. This is how I finally got my start as a salesman, the highest paid professional on Earth, as well as an engineer, the alleged creator of all products, in the financial capital of the world, New York City.

"THE ENTREPRENEUR IS NOT REALLY INTERESTED IN DOING THE WORK; HE IS INTERESTED IN CREATING THE WAY THE COMPANY OPERATES. IN THAT REGARD, THE ENTREPRENEUR IS AN INVENTOR. HE OR SHE LOVES TO INVENT, BUT DOES NOT LOVE TO MANUFACTURE OR SELL OR DISTRIBUTE WHAT HE OR SHE INVENTS."

- MICHAEL GERBER

THE LABORATORY

&

"IMAGINATION IS MORE IMPORTANT THAN KNOWLEDGE."
- ALBERT EINSTEIN

It took a year, some luck, and a very inflated resume to land my first real job with Canon USA, the world famous maker of cameras. Rich Chereskin fell in like with me when the interview turned from my experience as a salesman, to his children and his love of "the game" of baseball.

Rich was a sports fanatic, as are most men in the competitive world of sales. They think every aspect of life is a game. His son, as I did years ago, was struggling on his baseball team. As did I, his son had not hit a pebble with his bat, much less a fast ball.

"So, you say even though my son is not doing well, I should continue to take him to practice?"

"Absolutely!" I replied enthusiastically. "When I was a kid, for about three seasons, I could not even hold the bat upright my wrists were so skinny. But one day, out of nowhere, I hit a single that turned into a triple before the dust settled. From that moment on, I was a madman at bat.

In the off season, my dad took me to the park and taught me to throw---really hard. When I came back in the spring, I terrorized the entire league as I was now used to throwing a ball with a man. We went straight to the championship. You will

75

see, if you stay at it, your son will do the same thing," I urged, lecturing him as if I was his manager. My big speech must have gone over well, because even though I failed terribly in those first few months, Rich would not allow anyone to fire me.

I was his favorite of the four engineers he hired and I wanted desperately to make him proud of his choice. What's more, I was so excited to finally have cards with my name on them and the title---engineer. Working for a famous company like Canon USA was just the icing on the cake.

To avoid pain, years earlier, Canon engineers used the four magic words of all creation and said, "Instead of using cameras to take pictures of people, what if we used it to take pictures of documents in the office?" They simply took their famous cameras and turned them into copy machines for business offices, as everyone knows, there is nothing absolutely new being created under the sun.

Copy machines had become hot commodities, as they were relieving the pain of losing time and energy or what business people call, efficiency, for companies of all sizes. Computer systems were doing the same thing and were quickly becoming hot commodities as well. Working together, computers and copy machines were a relationship made in heaven.

Rich hired me to help his salespeople sell computers to their many long-time camera and copy machine customers. Their salespeople worried about selling the copy machines and my job was to sell their customers a computer system in a package deal. My job title was Sales Engineer because I was designing, as well as selling the computer systems. There were four of us. We were their hired technical guns.

Four engineers were hired because we could process, or had access to unlimited amounts of information about computers and how they could protect companies from painfully losing lots of money. The copier salespeople had already earned the complete trust of their clients and for this, we were allowed to come in and talk about our hot commodity, computers.

I tagged along with all the copier salespeople to their meetings in the hopes of convincing the president that their employees would make them a lot more money in less time, using less energy, if they just bought everyone a new computer. If I made a sale, I got a commission. The copier salesperson that brought me to meet their client, also made a healthy commission just for the introduction.

I did not realize how lucky I was then, but years later, care of Rich Chereskin, I saw how my first real job had placed a completely assembled money machine right in my lap to play with. In my ignorance, I spent the next 20 years searching for it relentlessly.

As a Sales Engineer, I was using information (Computer System Design) to sell computers with copy machines, which helped me to develop strong relationships with my internal customers, the copier salespeople (CS), as well as my external customers that purchased our products. These relationships produced money and most importantly, more information (feedback), as our customers told us how they believed we could better make and sell the computers and copiers once they purchased them.

Success = CSD + (Computers & Copy Machines) + (CS & Customers) = **$$$ & Feedback**

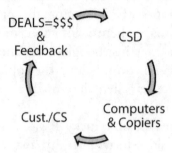

Rich built a money machine for us using one of the most powerful brands of information to sell in all of business, gossip, or what others call, the word of mouth. He said, "Bintell, once you get your first sale, large or small, that news will spread like wildfire throughout the entire branch. If you play your cards right, all 100 copier salespeople will bring you to meet their best customers. If things work the way we think they will, you will have tons of sweet deals thrown in your lap before you know what hit you. You may even have to hire an assistant?"

"They've got to be joking! Me, with an assistant?" I thought. I was excited and raring to go.

Success = Gossip + (Me & Computers) + (Customers & Copier Salespeople) = **$$$**

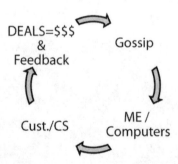

In the beginning, things were slow, and I mean really slow, but I kept my head down and learned as much as I could about computer systems. The information I had about computers and how they could help companies make money faster, with less work, was really the only thing I brought to the table. The copier salespeople had the trusted customer relationships, and it was my job to provide a wealth of information to sell the computers to close deals. If everything went as planned, success for me was just a matter of time.

Rich was right. After that first sale, the news spread throughout the branch like a forest fire. I would come walking into the office and get run over by copier salespeople, anxious to make easy money. They suddenly needed me for this appointment that was a "sure thing," or that meeting that was already a "done deal." Computers were not the only hot commodity I had to keep track of, as now, people were buying me. My time became just as, if not more valuable than the computers I was selling.

When I walked into meetings set up by the copier salesman, all I had to do was share some information about computer systems and how they could make a company more money, when they worked together with copy machines. After a few sentences, the president of the company would say, "Okay Mr. Powell, what do we need to get started?" There were months when I would leave with $30,000 in commissions on top of my regular salary. It was more money than I had ever dreamed I would see in my young sales career.

If I wanted to make more money, all I had to do was add more copier salespeople and some additional computer equipment. When I finally stumbled upon this formula years later, I was inspired to write this book when I realized one of the richest men in the world, Michael Bloomberg, began his journey selling computers in New York City. He is now the Mayor of New York and in 2009, his wealth was reported at over $16 billion. With valuable relationships all over the world, he is listed as one of the top 10 most powerful men on Earth. He too was an engineer.

The product I was selling meant nothing really. I could have been selling paint and paintbrushes, or crayons with coloring books. The money machine designed by my managers worked flawlessly. By the end of the year, Rich was as proud of me as he would have been of his own son. I got my money machine working so well, I won an all expense paid trip to one of the wealthiest places on Earth, Monte Carlo's South of France. I thought I was on top of the world and then, things changed.

IN THIS LIFE, THE ONLY THING THAT IS PREDICTABLE, IS THE UNPREDICTABILITY OF HOW FAST THINGS CAN AND WILL CHANGE.

WAKE UP CALL

&

After a while, the copier people became uncomfortable, as they felt I was making too pretty a penny off of their hard work. My over confident attitude probably did not help the situation either. Looking back, I ran the money machine Rich handed me right into the ground.

With the copier people bringing me deals, I really did not have to do much of anything most days. Other than talking to people once or twice a day, it really was an easy job. Many days, I did not even have to go to the office. I got so good at delivering my wealth of information, I closed most deals over the phone.

But when the bickering about Bintell not coming to the office reached a boiling point throughout the branch, I was so ashamed and upset, I could not even face Rich. In an emotional decision that I regret to this day, I decided to go out on my own, as I wanted to prove to them, as well as myself, that I could stand on my own two feet. Boy, I sure was wrong!

Without those trusted copier salespeople introducing me to their customers, I had to make hundreds of calls each day to find clients of my own. When I tried to call old customers without the copier people knowing, they always asked about their trusted copy machine salesperson. When they found out we were no longer working as a team, all the trust went right out the door. My calls usually ended on some ones voicemail machine and not returned.

Failure = CSD + (ME & Computers) + ~~Relationships~~ = **$0.00**

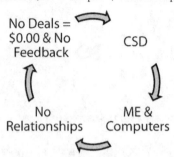

On my own, selling computer systems was a painfully slow process. I considered going back to school, or changing my profession completely, but one day a high school friend who had become a lawyer gave me a much needed pep talk. He said, "You think another college degree is the answer to all your problems? I own my own law firm, and many days, I feel like a used car salesman the way my lawyer buddies and I pass each other clients."

I slowed down and thought about what he said. If the lawyers were just like me and the copier salesman passing each other clients, there had to be a universal law that we could all use to make our lives easy. Something obvious. Something basic. Something like a formula.

FORMULAS ARE THE MOST RELIABLE MACHINES KNOWN TO MAN. THEY ALWAYS WORK, AND THEY NEVER, EVER, BREAK DOWN.

DEJA VU

&

NECESSITY IS THE MOTHER OF ALL INVENTION.

The thought of a universal formula that produced success reminded me of one day back in college playing hooky from a lab class, and following a friend into an economics class, hoping to learn something about money.

As I sat in the back of the class hiding, listening to this professor talk about the cause of unemployment throughout a country, I was shocked to see this economics professor use the same formula to calculate the pace of inflation, my engineering professor used to calculate the amount of electricity flowing through a wire. It was my first taste of how formula's can be used successfully, in more places than just one.

So when my lawyer friend made the comments about how he and his buddies pass each other clients, which sounded exactly like my job as a Sales Engineer, I felt a chill run up my spine, as my guitar teacher way back in 4th grade once told me to always pay strict attention to anything that repeats.

Even still, the 10 years that followed as a lone salesman with no copier salespeople to introduce me to their customers were rocky ones to put it lightly. Somehow I survived 10 years of being hired, and then six months later, only to be fired for a lack of sales. The only success I was able to find and save myself from complete financial destruction, was through my ability to sell myself and land yet another job.

Success = (Info. to sell) + (ME) + (Employer) = **Job**

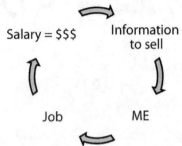

For years, I interviewed well, convincing employers of my willingness to work hard. I was a commodity being purchased by employers who saw me as a product that could save them time and energy, just like the computers I was selling. If a hiring manager acted as if I could not do the job, I would say, "Sir, engineers are the people that make these products. Selling them is the easy part." My friends called me The Great Interviewer.

All the companies were after the same thing. They already had what they believed to be a valuable commodity. All they needed me to do was use the information I had to turn it into a hot one. From my experience with Canon USA, I felt I could do the job.

We were both partially right. I did have the information part, but the relationship department was where I was lacking. Without a constant stream of customers being introduced to me by copier salespeople, sales were few and far between and I was fired in six months every time, like clockwork.

Even though I always managed to find another job, my self esteem suffered greatly. A few times I ran into hard financial troubles and ended up back on my mother's couch, practically homeless. Others who had chosen safer, stable career paths, caught up to the $280,000 salary I became a master at negotiating, but never collecting and were passing me now by leaps and bounds.

They were buying homes in nice neighborhoods and

even raising their families. Shame enveloped me as I could not support anyone with a six month salary each year. My student loans went unpaid. Disaster seemed to be the inevitable.

I felt like giving up on my hopes and dreams of being an international businessman completely, but if others could do it, so could I. Besides, if I changed career paths now and accepted failure, all I had learned would have been for nothing. I slowed down, took a deep breath and luckily, an idea came to mind.

SUCCESS IS A POINT IN TIME WHERE PREPARATION AND OPPORTUNITY COLLIDE.

U-TURN

I fell back on what had worked for me in the past like a soft feathered down comforter, partnering with other salespeople selling products that complimented mine. If I was selling computers, and they were selling keyboards, we were the best of friends.

After I had my partners waiting in the wings, I went to my manager and asked him to help me with the golden rule of all business. I knew that before the partners would really get excited about helping me, they needed to know one thing. "What's in it for me?" Meaning, "How much money will you pay me on the deals I bring you?"

Success = Selling Info + (ME + Commodity + Money for Partners) + Partners = **$$$**

Deals =
$$$

Info that
Sells

ME &
Commodity &
Pay Out to
Partners

Channel
Partners

I thought my manager was going to say, "Why should we pay someone else to do your job?" But he did not. Surprisingly, before I could finish explaining my big plan, without blinking an eye, he said, "How much do we need to pay your people to get them to start working with us?"

When I told some of the other, older salespeople about my ingenious plan to re-invent myself, they said, "Everyone does that Bintell. They are called channel partners. I have about 20 of them myself. It is the only way I can survive. The companies I have worked for did not pay me hundreds of thousands because I was necessarily smarter than the next person. They pay me because my partners and their customers trust me to tell them the truth about anything I sell. I am the product they are purchasing, and with that, they will buy whatever I tell them to. These relationships are so strong, not even money can buy them!"

Soon I did not have to make hundreds of calls each day, as the partners I had would call and tell me which company needed what, and exactly who I should call to get a deal signed. All I had to do was pay the partner their fee when the deals closed, or send them a deal in return to keep them happy. When one partner sent me a lead I knew was right for another, I passed it to them. We were like one big happy family. It worked just as smoothly, many times even better than when I was a Sales Engineer.

> When happy customers bring business to a company they purchased a commodity from, it's called a referral. Companies usually pay for referrals

Without the threat of losing my job in six months hanging over my head, I bought myself enough time to see exactly how the largest and most powerful companies in the world worked from their mailrooms, right up to the president's office. The more I saw, the more I realized that what made them successful, was exactly what had made me a success as a Sales Engineer, and now as a businessman on my own.

Conversations about billion dollar companies that started from a simple paperclip and grew into them selling washers and dryers that before seemed like complex, high level discussions way above my head, were suddenly simply a function of ***The***

Formula spinning around and around. When wealthy business men talked on television, I would sit listening for the information part, the commodity part, and the relationship part, and they were always there. One of the most fascinating success stories I heard was Ralph Lauren's.

Ralph Lauren began his career in fashion in 1968 selling his own type of ties to department stores. He said, "Instead of a plain tie, what if I put additional information to sell it right on the tie itself? What if I put my logo on it?" From that first mega-success selling that one commodity, he now owns a multi-billion dollar worldwide clothing empire / lifestyle brand that sells everything from suits to underwear to home furnishings. He has a personal net worth of $6 billion. He is known as one of the greatest businessmen ever and he started his extraordinary career as of all things, a salesman.

BEGAN IN 1968   PRESENT

$$$ + Feedback	Type 1, 2 & 3 for RL Ties	National Distribution = Millions + Feedback	Feedback = Type 1, 2 & 3 info for full Clothing Line	Worldwide Distribution = Billions + Feedback	Feedback = Type 1, 2 & 3 info for full Lifestyle Brand
Local Retail Stores	RL Ties with RL Logo on the tie itself	National Retail Stores & Celebrity Models	Full Clothing Line. Private RL Retail Stores & Him Himself	Worldwide Retail Stores & Celebrity Models	Full Clothing Line. Private RL Retail Stores & Him

Excited about this fool proof method for success, I ran to tell one of my best friends. He had been through similar, if not worse ups and downs in his sales career. But to my surprise, he was not impressed in the least with my new found formula for success, even though he agreed that it did indeed work. He said, "Bintell, I am tired of all this. I do not want to deal with this pressure anymore. I just want a paycheck that I can count on." Two weeks later, he took a job paying close to minimum wage as a bus driver. For months, his choice confused me. Then, it hit me.

Although I felt strongly that success was guaranteed in my formula, he felt success was guaranteed in the arms of a paycheck, care of the rat race. Even after I had given him the formula for success, he chose to quit. Even after I told him about the multi-million dollar deals I was closing, he did not seem to care. That was when I knew, success was made of something simpler than the reliable money machine I now had in my possession.

Success really had nothing to do with my engineering degree, or my ability to deliver information, the computer systems I sold, or the partners I came to realize I needed so desperately to prosper. Success began with a simple thing inside us all. An infinitely valuable thing we all must come to grips with on our own terms. Without this thing, this success formula, this revolving money machine, as valuable as it appears, is absolutely worthless.

Later on, learning that Li Ka Shing, the richest man in all of China, a fugitive who fled Hong Kong as the Japanese invaded China, started building an empire that reaches into 40 countries and accounts for 11 percent of the Hong Kong's Stock Market, as a salesman selling plastic plants, convinced me that success was free to the public, the world, and even me.

Success was not about being short, or tall, good looking or unattractive, smart or maybe not so smart. True success was made of something far simpler than I would have ever guessed. The answer to all the success I could ever wish for was waiting for me, way back in elementary school, given to me by my elementary school teacher on my last day of class. His words of wisdom would be the greatest graduation present I would ever receive.

WISDOM IS STORED INFORMATION ONE CAN PULL FROM MEMORY TO PRODUCE A SUCCESSFUL OUTCOME; SORT OF LIKE A FORMULA.

ACT FIVE

Success = Information + Commodities + Relationships = $$$

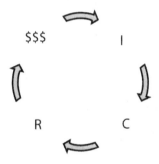

HUMAN CURRENCY

THE GREAT CHOICE

&

LIFE ON EARTH CAN BE SUMMED UP AS HUMAN BEINGS
PROCESSING INFORMATION, AND THEN MAKING
CHOICES TO AVOID PAIN.

> *"At a certain point, we just had to will this thing to happen."*
> Howard Shultz—CEO Starbucks Coffee

It was my 6th grade year and my teacher was a big tall burly man with a thick black beard named Mr. Gullucio. He was a full time teacher, part time aspiring Opera singer. His graduation gift to the entire class was a love for the world of movies, plays and acting. Mr. Gullucio's nickname for me was "Little Mouse."

He would call me Mouse and pat my shoulder with affection in his eyes whenever he caught me doing something I should not have. I never understood why he chose that name for me until graduation day finally came around.

Three weeks into our first semester, Mr. Gullucio marched the entire class down to the school auditorium in his usual flamboyant style and made a major announcement.

"Class, I am bringing you here today because you are going to do something very special for the entire student body the day before you graduate from elementary, and move onto your new life in the junior high." As Mr. Gullucio spoke and sashayed back and forth on the stage, his deep voice held us all in mid air, speechless, hanging off of his every word.

"We are going to perform the play Guys & Dolls for the entire school and we are going to hold auditions---TODAY!" he rumbled. The entire class broke into cheer. We clapped and hugged each other in excitement. Someone was helping us to be important. It was like the choice to be successful had already been taken care of by our fearless leader. We would be stars by year's end. The very next week, we took our first field trip to the Metropolitan Opera House in Manhattan to see Carmen performed live.

Mr. Gullucio must have known I really needed to be popular because he gave me a starring role as Big Julie, the feared gangster who had the entire cast trembling when he walked into the room. Although many teachers had written me off as a distant young man with potential, who did not want to do much more than eat candy all day, he gave me the world as if I was entitled to it without a second thought.

Many days we would skip our studies and rehearse for the play all day. Ironically, I read more. The repetition of performing the lines of the script made reading through my school work a lot easier. The words began rolling off my tongue without much thought after a while. The more I practiced my lines, the more people believed and clapped when we rehearsed them. It felt powerful. Like the words were alive.

Well, the big night came and went off in Emmy winning fashion. My entire family, along with the entire student body witnessed me pull off a leading role in the biggest event of the school year. With the entire audience smiling and clapping as I took my final bow, I learned then, under the hot stage lights, that the success that comes from popularity, not only made me confident and calm, but was also powerful.

The next day, Mr. Gullucio gave us our report cards. I was used to getting C's and D's with a few B's scattered around in subjects like gym and art. This semester, I was delighted to see A's, some B's and only one C. No D's and no F's. Excited to show an adult my fine work, I ran over to Mr. Gullucio and showed him what I had achieved as if he had no knowledge of it. I was expecting praise. Instead, I got the shock of my life.

"Mr. Gullucio, look. I got A's, B's and only one C. I did good right?" He looked down at me, and for the first time in our year long history, he shot me the same harsh look my mother had given me on too many occasions. He said, "Bintell, who are we fooling here? You chose to get those grades and nothing better the first day you stepped foot in my class. Others chose to get better grades and they got them, but you, for some odd reason chose to settle only for B's. You and I both know you could have done much better, if you chose to."

My heart sank in my chest and I felt a tear well up in my right eye. I loved Mr. Gullucio because he was the one person who treated me like an adult. He always gave me the benefit of the doubt, even when I did not act like an adult. Now, suddenly, being an adult was not as much fun as it had been before. I wanted to be a child again. Before I could pick my heart up off the floor, Mr. Gullucio put his hand on my shoulder and spoke to me as lovingly as my grandmother would. He said, "Bintell, do you know why I call you Mouse?"

"No," I replied with my head down, too ashamed to look him in the eyes.

"Because I've watched you make bad choices at times, and I have proudly watched you make good ones throughout this entire year. I have watched you like an energetic little mouse scurrying around in this maze of a classroom. Every time you have made good choices, it has warmed my heart. On the other hand, I have hoped you learned valuable lessons from your poor choices. We all have special gifts in life. All your classmates have their gifts and you have one too. I see it. I am hoping that after this year, you will too. You can be anything you choose to put your mind to. Success is a choice Bintell. Promise me you will never be afraid to make the choice to succeed. Okay? Promise me!"

I shook my head yes and Mr. Gullucio smiled and patted me on the shoulder, then he sashayed away the way he did when he proudly walked our class through the hallways each day. I stood there speechless, watching him, knowing I was seeing one of the most important people in my life walk away from me, maybe for the last time. Would I forget his words? Would I choose success or failure? With this information, what could possibly stop me?

WHEN MUHAMMAD ALI AND JOE FRAZIER MET IN THE FAMED FIGHT OF THE CENTURY, FRAZIER WAS THE UNDERDOG. PEOPLE SAID HE COULD NOT WIN AS ALI WAS JUST TOO FAST AND TOO STRONG. WHEN THEY INTERVIEWED FRAZIER HE SAID, "NO MATTER WHAT, I AM NOT GOING DOWN!" FRAZIER WENT ON TO WIN THAT FIGHT AFTER ENDURING EXTREME PUNISHMENT.

THERE ARE SUCCESSFUL PEOPLE THAT WERE DESTINED TO BE, BUT THERE ARE MANY MORE THAT WERE DETERMINED TO BE.

SUCCESS IS A CHOICE TO SUCCEED.

GAS MONEY

&

"IF MONEY IS YOUR HOPE FOR INDEPENDENCE, YOU WILL NEVER HAVE IT. THE ONLY REAL SECURITY THAT A MAN WILL HAVE IN THIS WORLD IS A RESERVE OF KNOWLEDGE, EXPERIENCE, AND ABILITY."
-HENRY FORD – REVOLUTIONIZED THE AUTOMOTIVE INDUSTRY

I left Mr. Gullucio's 6th grade class excited to enjoy my summer vacation, armed with a new sense of purpose. My first summer assignment was to tag along with my parents as they attempted to get their piece of the good life with a whirlwind trip to Europe.

They seemed to call a financial timeout, and for two whole weeks they stopped arguing over money as we took the most extravagant trip of our humble lives. This confused me to no end as suddenly, out of nowhere, we were living as if we were rich people. We did not have money to get candy bars from the grocery store check-out counter, but we had money for this?

We took the Concord to visit my Aunt Cybil living in England who became our tour guide for night flights to Paris; the hovercraft to see the White Shores of Dover and rides in sports cars with weird sounding names at high speeds on the Autobahn, while my sister and I screamed in the back seat, "That's my car!"

All this as I read every comic book I could get my hands on and watched my father like a hawk, as he strutted about in the grey wool pinstriped suit my mother purchased for him the day before we left. He looked just like the successful men I would see on television, which convinced me that somehow, surely, my humble family would survive the stress and strain of our money woes and stay together. Unfortunately, I was wrong.

The whole time we were on our whirlwind vacation, Aunt Cybil kept going on and on about all the new friends she had made living in England. She seemed to be impressed with them all, but one of her new friends had a leg up on everyone.

This one young woman from an area close to where my mother had grown up was the topic of discussion for the entire trip. Aunt Cybil went on and on about how her friend's son was so passionate about playing the guitar. It seemed as though she would never stop explaining how he was regarded as a genius, not to mention all his musical talent at such a young age. She drove the point home completely, which caused my mother to frown at me because, I hated my guitar.

Every Saturday morning my mother would wake me up at the crack of dawn and drag me to guitar lessons with this old drill sergeant in his dimly lit dining room. He would correct me every two seconds for this reason, that one and the other. For years this dragged on.

After practice, my mother would drive me home while she lectured about how I should take my studies serious. I would go upstairs to my room, lie on my bed facing the ceiling with my guitar on my stomach and strum it for an hour to convince her I was practicing so she would let me go outside and play. She was intent on turning me into some sort of musical wizard, while I was intent on winning the admiration of my friends by playing touch football whenever the traffic allowed. My mother and I clashed on this topic for years.

After all the ups and downs in grade school with teachers that tested me on subjects I had no interest in, and with all the older guitar teachers who forced me to play music from their era, which I could not relate to, the guitar was the last thing on my mind. I could not use it to make myself popular, so I just knew I was anything but passionate, or talented and only God knows what a genius was, so I definitely was not that.

As Aunt Cybil uttered the words again and again, talent, passion and genius hit me in the heart and soul of my confidence and self esteem like a shot gun blast, dragging out of me whatever self respect Mr. Gullucio's words had put there less than a week ago. I sat in the back of the rental car we were driving on the Autobahn, hiding myself in a comic book while my sister played with her Barbie Dolls, trying to ignore my aunt's voice as best I could.

After years of yelling and punishments, my mother finally gave into the fact that the guitar and I would just never be a match made in heaven. I stopped playing for years. My guitar and case somehow found its way to the bottom of my closet, with old dirty sneakers worn to the soles lying on top of it. Whenever I opened my closet and saw it, I felt like a failure. It was a reminder of my lack of passion, talent and genius, whatever that was. I wanted to throw it away but I just could not bring myself to do it.

When my college years came rolling into view, I am ashamed to admit that academics was not the most important thing in my eyes. Because my family had moved around for as long as I can remember, I was left with a large void in the friendship department. As a result, my social life was at the top of my priority list.

There were all sorts of interesting people in college who had earned scholarships in sports or academics, and with the Berkeley School of Music just around the corner, I met quite a few young people with scholarships in music as well. Being the engineering major, most of these people who seemed to be full of personality and excitement, were in classes I would never attend, driving a bigger wedge between me and my dreams of social acceptance. Luckily, there was one guy from New York, very popular, not just on campus, but throughout Boston, who ended up in one of my only two economics classes.

His name was Steven and everyone loved him. Steven even had the president of the college eating out of his hands. He seemed to know everything about anything, as he had traveled the world with his family before landing on Northeastern University's campus. Steven lived in an apartment while most people lived on campus. He was on the crew team and had a convertible sports car, which made him a bit of a superstar.

He saw me as an engineering project, amused by all I had not been exposed to I guess. Steven and his girlfriend took me to restaurants that served raw fish, to his parent's beach house to water-ski, to all sorts of movies and to parties on every campus in the Boston area. Many days I would skip my classes to hang out in his, just so I would not miss out on any of the fun.

One day I made the mistake of telling Steven how much I hated playing my guitar as a kid. He and his girlfriend Liz were in love with every type of music imaginable. This caused them to take me to a concert in Harvard Square that changed everything I previously thought about playing the guitar that now lay in a pile of dust back home, at the bottom of my messy closet.

As I sat there flabbergasted, watching this wizard play his guitar just as well as I could speak words from my own mouth, I was immediately reminded of our famous family trip years ago and how Aunt Cybil had gone on and on about the incredible talent of her friend's son on his guitar. She obviously had not seen this young man playing, as if ever there was someone with passion, talent, and whatever it was to be a genius, it had to be him.

He played up and down the neck of the entire guitar the way my teachers had begged me to. He played slow, fast and everything in between. He seemed to be discovering new ways of playing his guitar right in front of us all, as he played songs by musician like The Beatles, my musical hero Miles Davis and songs he had written himself.

I left the concert speechless, ashamed of myself for wasting all those years mindlessly strumming my guitar in my room. Not a word left my mouth as we rode back to campus. It was the first time I felt intense pangs of passion about anything, of all things my guitar.

I made a choice that night in the back of his car that not even the pain of a thousand deaths would stop me from learning to play my guitar the way I had seen the wizard play that evening. I would live to hear people call me talented when I played that guitar if it was the last thing I ever did. Maybe I would even find out what a genius was along the way.

Steven and Liz did not understand what I was going through and I did not try to explain. My behavior must have been very scary, as it was the last time they ever offered to take me anywhere. Luckily for me, the experience turned my entire life around, and just in the nick of time.

PASSION IS THE FUEL FOR YOUR SUCCESS / MONEY MACHINE.

A NEW BEGINNING

&

BEING A GENIUS IS JUST LIKE MAKING FRUIT PUNCH.

On any given day, I was the weird guy walking through Northeastern University's campus with my school books in one arm, and my guitar in the other. I played my guitar and studied for engineering classes tirelessly. After failing classes and taking incompletes to avoid D's and F's, I had a lot of catching up to do.

In an effort to reclaim wasted time, I took seven, sometimes eight classes a semester when the prescribed limit was four. I juggled playing in the school jazz band with double the engineering class workload and surprisingly, I received nothing less than a B that semester. I was stunned. My mother was all smiles. My father was speechless.

In one year, taking double the workload, I caught up and finally managed to graduate. It felt like my head was close to spinning off my shoulders from all the information the professors stuffed into it. This degree of information was labeled a Bachelors of Science in Electrical Engineering.

Back home in New York, with the memory of the guy from Harvard Square playing his guitar like a magician still vivid in my memory, I looked for engineering jobs during the day and practiced my guitar all night in famous Jazz clubs like The Blue

Note and The Village Vanguard.

After playing songs over and over, I came up with my own little ways of speaking on my guitar, just like the guy from the concert a year ago. Later on, I learned these little ways of speaking on the guitar that reminded me so much of formulas from my engineering classes, were called riffs.

Riffs were just like formulas, as they worked in any musical situation I found myself in. Addicted to the success they provided, I went crazy making and memorizing as many of them as possible. Using the four magic words to create them I asked myself, "Instead of playing the melody like that, what if I played it like this?"

Throughout my musical journey, I learned that musicians had formulas, just like engineers did. In the world of engineering, our formulas are mathematical, while in the world of music, the formulas are melodious.

> "Success is doing what you love and would do without pay every minute, hour and day of your life"
> Tommy Hilfiger

Musicians used scales, chord changes, arpeggios, melodies, blues, AABA song models, and my personal favorite, riffs. Musicians memorized these melodious formulas that worked perfectly in all musical situations and after a while, they began to come up with their own, as I now was, just like I had watched my magician friend do. For once, formulas were not tedious, they were fun.

I felt vindicated when people called me of all things, passionate and talented on my guitar. In an act that would have made my mother proud, I looked up the word passion to get its meaning, as the word had intimidated me for most of my young life. The dictionary said passion was any powerful or compelling emotion or feeling, like love, hate, or anger.

The definition cleared things up a bit, as I was in love with music. I ate, slept and breathed it. It consumed me as I had little or no interest in much of anything else. Whatever relationships I did have at that time were just as captivated by music as I was. After years of sleeping my days away, I was interested in anything but sleep, as this passion thing, in music at least, was keeping me up all night.

Then one late night while trying to write my first song on my sister's piano, half watching a show about the famous billionaire clothing designer Ralph Lauren, I heard a definition for genius that opened my eyes to the world of creation and invention, in a way all the engineering classes I took in school had not.

Her name was Angela Davis. She was a flamboyant fashion critic who was now an editor for a prestigious magazine. While commenting on the runway show she said, "The true definition of a genius is a person who can take separate pieces of information about products already available, they can rearrange this information, and present it back to people as a product, that adds value to millions of lives, and is current to the time period they are living in or better yet --- timeless."

I sat there speechless, as Ms. Davis had finally cleared up a world of pain, insecurity and confusion which stretched back as far as I could remember. With her definition for genius replaying in my head, I took a deep breath. Finally, I knew what a genius was. I no longer felt like I had to bow my head and beg the pardon of those who were considered geniuses.

Being a genius was not this fictitious God-given gift that only a choice few were blessed to be born with. Anyone could be a genius. You did not have to be an engineer to take one or two products already available to people and combine them into a "new" one. The whole world was instantly a creation playground where anyone could play the genius game and win.

It was like the old products were coming together and creating the new ones. New products were practically making themselves. Being a genius was just like making fruit punch. Instead of just drinking orange juice, what if we add some apple juice, and then add a dab of grapefruit juice, and there you are, fruit punch.

New sneakers with roller-skating wheels inside the soles,

pencils with double the eraser on the end, three minute movies for songs called music videos, tattoos on tee-shirts, spray bottles with butter, musicians using old styles of singing and covering them in modern day drum beats and riffs.

Somehow I managed to land a job as a Sales Engineer. In the years that followed, caught right in the middle of the rat race, I kept one eye on ingenious products that were purchased by enough people to become hot commodities, and the other eye on the people that created them. The computer world was bubbling with genius, as the computer engineers were constantly asking themselves the big, "Instead of... what if?" question.

I could not believe how simple the creation process that was driving the entire world of computers actually was. "Instead of having separate computers on each desk, what if we connected them so they can communicate and share information quickly? Then they said, "Instead of letting people and computers talk over the wires we talk on phones with, what if we cleaned up this mess of wires and did it all over the radio?"

> "Beyond talent lie all the usual words: discipline, love, luck—but, most of all, endurance"
> James Arthur Baldwin

They did not stop there either. They continued by asking themselves, "Instead of using the radio, what if we did it over the Internet because it's free?" Then, when I thought they could not do anything more, they said, "Instead of just talking over the Internet, what if we put movies, television and face-to-face meetings all over the Internet, all in an attempt to save time and energy?" Then, they started the entire process over, this time using cellular phones.

Everyone was moving forward with the "what if" question. Genius was bubbling over everywhere making people from all walks of life very, very rich. I found genius in everything from music, to art, to kitchen utensils, to cars that ran on electricity and gas called hybrids.

Talk show host that interviewed these special people able to create new hot commodities, or turn themselves into one, always spoke about them in exactly the same way Aunt Cybil had talked about the famous guitar player so many years before. Passion, talent and genius were always the words used to describe them. The three terms had to be somehow connected.

Passion had given me the energy to stay up, night after night for hours on end, gathering as much melodious information about how I could create my new found love of musical formulas, the riff. It turned me into a tireless, musical information collecting and processing machine. Without passion, just the thought of my guitar bored me, putting me right to sleep.

In a one-on-one interview, the world famous designer Carolina Herrera, who was never formally trained in design school said, "There is no way I could do what I do if I was not passionate about it. Just the amount of time I put into it would make it impossible if I did not feel passionate about what I was doing."

After about a year of listening to so many success stories about people from so many different walks of life talking about their passion in the same way, I was sure that passion energized people to spend all their time collecting enough information to dream up— a hot commodity.

But there was still the talent part. What was it exactly? Talented people worth millions and billions were worshiped like gods on television and in magazines, so talent had to be important. How did information tie talent, genius and passion together? Where was the connection?

$$SUCCESS = I + C + R$$

SUCCESS → PASSION

GENIUS ← TALENT

YOU CAN TRADE HARD LABOR FOR DOLLARS, OR IDEAS FOR BILLIONS.

TALENT POOL

&

> *"I've missed more than 9000 shots in my career. I've lost almost 300 games. 26 times, I've been trusted to take the game winning shot and missed. I've failed over and over and over in my life. This is why I succeed." Michael Jordan*

YOUR TALENT MAKES YOU THE HOT COMMODITY

My obsession with talent continued right past my triumphant entry into the rat race. In between all night jam sessions and jobs that lasted six months on average, using high priced things to disguise myself as an already very successful young man, I managed to socialize with the most talented people the New York City social scene had to offer.

Ten years flew by as I frequented art gallery openings, world championship celebratory events for successful basketball, football and baseball teams, designer perfume and champagne launch parties, music release parties, fashion shows and star studded celebrity birthday parties. These events came equipped with thousands of mere mortals offering these ultra successful people just about anything, dying to develop relationships with them.

While I paid for everything, they paid for nothing. They would get goody bags full of the latest and greatest in new commodities soon to hit the stores. Their creators requested payment with only a promise that they would use their products in public. At these talent-driven social events, people stepped aside so these successful people could enter with ease, while I had to wait in line unless I was with one of them. They were paid hundreds of thousands of dollars just to simply make an appearance, while I paid top dollar for entry. They had people offering them more success at such alarming rates, they hired bodyguards to stop the flow of success chasing after them.

While my parents and everyone I knew went off kicking and screaming about how the rat race was not giving them this, that and the other, the rat race chased after these "celebrities" relentlessly, offering them everything just shy of the world. Watching their money machines work was like watching a fairy tale dream about success falling from the sky.

They had success chasing them in such abundance, they were running from it, hiding even. The word talent was everywhere every single one of them was. Their talent seemed to turn them into worldwide hot commodities.

"He or she is so young and so talented," was the most common comment. When young golf professionals won a Masters Tournament, people would say, "His parents must be so proud as the world watches this young talent receive the highest honor in all of golf." Some of these special people took this talent thing a step further and were known to the world as "multi-talented." Every time anyone talked about talented people, their age always made their talent that much more impressive. It was as if time and talent were somehow tied together.

Singers were talented with long promising careers ahead of them. Athletes were so talented, they skipped college and went straight into the pros. Young talented actors that won Oscars for breakthrough performances were worshiped and adored by the world, and clothing designers were so blessed, their clothing was proof of their incredible genius at such an early age. I feared my chance to be talented was slipping away with each passing day.

I tried once more to look up talent in the dictionary hoping to get lucky, but this time I was not successful.

Talent in the dictionary's words was something people did well or better than others. That was obvious. I needed to know why talented people were always worshiped for being so young. What role did time play in their talent and success?

Then one rainy day, stuck inside the house watching

television, the guy who had been terrified of the three little words, ashamed that he could never be talented, or passionate, and God only knew I would never be anything remotely resembling a genius, had an unlikely stroke of genius of his very own. A simple definition for talent came to me while I watched a commentator talk about Roger Federer winning a major tennis title for the fifth time.

The commentator was talking the viewing audience through a slow motion replay of Mr. Federer striking the ball. He said, "Look at his concentration. The way he has his eyes on the ball. His form and his text book mechanics. It is as if he is a tennis-playing machine, the way he processes information at such a fast pace. His mental and physical talent level is so far above the competitions, it is not funny."

As soon as the commentator said the three words information, talent, and machine in the same sentence, I knew my search for talent's meaning was over. I replayed all the interviews of successful people I had ever watched on television in the past year to test my new found definition for talent, the same way I would test for electricity through a wire in a lab class.

Every single person I read about or watched receive awards and endless praise on television for being talented, could process information, and then act on it, either mentally, or physically, or both, in a way that produced a successful outcome, in the shortest amount of time. That was talent!

Singers I had seen perform with little to no preparation and deliver musical information to a crowd, moving people to tears, were truly talented. Baseball players in their first time at bat, crushing the first 100 mile per hour pitch hurled at them, could process information about the speed of the ball and its position, swinging their bat to hit home-runs, over, and over, and over were physically, as well as mentally, talented.

Investors that could process information within minutes from the past, comparing it to information from the present, and pick stocks that made themselves and their clients millions of dollars were talent worth paying millions for. The actor that could read their lines just once, and go on stage in front of millions to deliver an Oscar winning performance on their first take was talented. World famous clothing designers that can take instructions one time and create a dress that lands their movie star clients on the front cover of every major magazine throughout the world are talented.

The best part about talent was, it could be grown. Like plants used fertilizer to grow, talent had its own fertilizer. All successful people used this thing to grow their talent over time. This talent-growing thing was free and readily available to the general public. My first run in with this thing occurred in my father's garage, one cold winter's night.

ECONOMISTS OF THE WORLD PUT SUCH A HIGH VALUE ON PASSION, TALENT AND GENIUS, THEY ARE REFERRED TO AS "HUMAN CURRENCY."

PASSION FRUIT

∞

"A MAN'S ERRORS ARE HIS/HER PORTAL OF DISCOVERY."
— JAMES JOYCE

My mother must have felt that getting an engineering degree was the only place to get my hands on all the secrets of talent, passion, and ingenious creation, so she masterminded my choice to become an engineer before I was old enough to know what I was getting myself into.

If I was not being dragged to guitar lessons, or painting lions and tigers in the kitchen with my sister, she would urge my father to take me into the garage and show me what made a car's engine work.

"Just take him into the garage and show him how the battery or how the brakes work," she begged. His argument was, "I don't want him to grow up and be a mechanic like me." Back then, I just wanted to be left alone to watch cartoons and eat ice cream. As always, she finally got her way.

One cold winter's night, my father walked me into the garage, lifted the hood and exposed the cars precious machine for my viewing pleasure. I climbed up the small ladder towards the front of the garage, and looked on thrilled as he unscrewed the metal cover of the engine's manifold.

With the heart and soul of the tireless machine that drove me to guitar lessons and my mother to the supermarket on weekends exposed, I felt like an engineer in training. I understood little. But what I did understand was the spinning pistons moving with the tireless repetition and precision of a very dependable machine. Its precision and dependability I knew could only be the product of one thing, a formula.

I watched my father open many car engines over the years, and when I got to college and began playing in the school's jazz band, there were days and nights filled with me practicing musical formulas over, and over, and over, tirelessly, just like the tireless engines I stared into as a boy. I would sit in a trance and watch my left hand dance on the neck of my guitar, just like the pistons danced around each other in the engines of my youth.

> On average it takes 7 attempts at a success to learn from your mistakes and then, find success

Some of the songs were difficult to play, and I made horrible mistakes trying to get through them. Determined to play like the magician from Harvard Square, I fought past my mistakes, ignoring the pain of teaching my fingers to play unfamiliar melodies until it sounded just right. After a while, there was no more pain. Soon I did not have to think about what I was playing. My hand played the songs on its own.

Stories of genius musicians like John Coltrane, notorious for practicing for days on end, making his instrument sound like of all things, a freight train, pushed me to practice until my fingertips bled.

One day while rehearsing for a concert, the leader of my college jazz band, in an attempt to motivate us said, "The great Dizzy Gillespie said one night before he was about to get on stage with his big band, that he learned more about playing music by making mistakes in front of people on stage, than he ever learned practicing for hours on end in his room alone." We all calmed down and the concert, which took place the very next day, went off in poetic fashion.

Years later, caught in the rat race, in a frantic quest to make money, I did the unthinkable. I once again put down my guitar, and pursued what I felt was a stable job in of all things, sales. The 10 years of losing my job every six months wiped away all I had discovered about passion, talent and genius, replacing it with pure shame.

Between the horrors of going from one job to the next, or blindly searching for new customers on the phone, I had countless managers tell me, "When you do not have your sales-pitch down pat, it takes 40 unsuccessful calls, to get that successful one. Learn from your failure and find that successful call before you leave for the day. You have 5 seconds to tell them what you can do for them. On the other side of your failure is success. Go get it!"

In spite of my manager's big speech, a few weeks later, I was let go from yet another sales job. In my frustrated and bewildered state, I looked for something to take my mind off of my failure. Luckily a high school friend, who had played music with me years before, took me to see Dizzy Gillespie play at my old stomping grounds, The Blue Note. Everyone was talking about his failing health. Most believed this was probably one of the last times the great co-creator of Bebop music would ever grace the stage.

In the front row I sat, watching the great master's trademark cheeks inflate as he played his trumpet and of all things, make mistakes. With the shame of losing yet another job heavy on my heart, and the memory of Dizzy's great words of wisdom regarding the value of mistakes, it finally dawned on me. Failure was actually valuable.

It was as if the dark night's sky opened up and a beam of light had come shining through. I had been ignoring my own life's journey, too embarrassed by my failures to learn anything from them. I was turning my back on my own growing pains, prolonging my success even further. Failure was just as important, if not more important to my success, than success itself.

When those drill sergeants of my musical past corrected my every mistake, I just wanted to give up. But later on, when I became passionate about music, my failures only made my desire to try again that much stronger, and with each repetitive act, my talent level increased, producing a brand new riff. Repetition was the fertilizer of my talent.

I was ignoring the priceless information that came from my own trial and error. This information was a model for what did not work, which was just as, if not more important to future successes than what did. The opposite of all my failures was the success I had been looking for. Failure is the mother of all creations four magic words. *Instead of* doing what does not work, *what if* we just do the exact opposite? Without failure, why would anyone ever ask the question, *"Instead of?"*

PASSION ➡ REPETITION ➡ TALENT ➡ GENIUS

Vincent Van Gogh, the famous father of impressionist painting, painted for days, energized by his passion, back and forth with brush strokes and different color mixtures. His talent grew so strong, he came across a stroke of genius and invented the vividly colorful impressionist style of painting. A failure of his time, he never sold one painting. Today, his paintings are sold for hundreds of millions of dollars.

Dizzy Gillespie, regarded as one of the best jazz trumpet player of all times, played his musical formulas over and over for hours, learning from his successes, as well as his failures, until his talent was so strong, he stumbled on a stroke of genius, inventing a style of music called Bebop. Michael Jordan, the best basketball player in the history of the game was cut from his high school basketball team. And the great Warren Buffett was denied entry to Harvard Business School. Luckily, all these people were in touch with their passion, because if they were not, they would never have achieved wild success, and they would not be role models for us today. I call this process of growing talent with passion, *The Passion Fruit.*

The Passion Fruit spins around and around, just like the pistons in a car engine. Each attempt at success produces information or what many call, ideas. The ideas that come out of this engine are made of four words.

"Instead of... What if?"

Once you have gathered enough information by asking yourself the creation question over and over and over, one failure and success at a time, the flood gates will open up, and that is when ingenious creations will come pouring out of you.

THE FORMULA AS THE PASSION FRUIT

Success = *"Instead of, what if"* + Commodities + Relationships = $$$

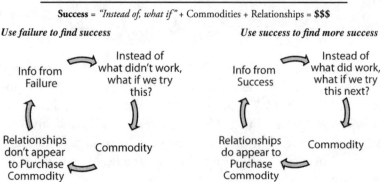

Use failure to find success

Info from Failure → Instead of what didn't work, what if we try this? → Commodity → Relationships don't appear to Purchase Commodity ↻

Use success to find more success

Info from Success → Instead of what did work, what if we try this next? → Commodity → Relationships do appear to Purchase Commodity ↻

Aware of the mistake of being so shamed of my failure, I looked around and found I was far from alone. It is understandable. Failure is not glorified on television and in magazines. Success is. But in this success-crazed society we live in, shame of facing failure causes us to make unconscious choices to fail again and again and again. It is not because we enjoy failure, but because we are deathly afraid of something else we believe is far more painful than failure. Some would rather fail forever, than face this thing. Then failure becomes habitual and comfortable.

It made sense of what the older sales veterans had complained about for years. One of the biggest stumbling blocks in selling customers anything new, even when they told me they needed it. The more I investigated this thing, the more I feared it. This thing was responsible for destroying multi-billion dollar empires in a matter of days. This thing was feared and respected by businessmen, CEOs and presidents throughout the world. This thing, can also make you rich overnight.

"NOTHING GREAT IN THIS WORLD HAS EVER BEEN ACHIEVED WITHOUT PASSION."
- CHRISTIAN FRIEDRICH HEBBEL - GERMAN POET

ACT SIX

Success = Information + Commodities + Relationships = $$$

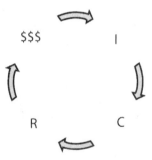

$$$ I

R   C

KING OF
PAIN

NO CHANGE, NO PAIN, NO GAIN

> *"Things do not change, people do."* Henry David Thoreau

> *"The successful person makes a habit of doing what the failing person doesn't like to do."* Thomas Edison

"CHANGE IS THE LAW OF LIFE. THOSE WHO LOOK ONLY TO THE PAST OR PRESENT ARE CERTAIN TO MISS THE FUTURE."

-JOHN F. KENNEDY

It is probably one of the most shameful moments of my life. I have never talked about it, or dared to tell anyone about it until now. Writing about it in this way is a frail attempt to clear my conscience and the shame I have lived with for years in making this choice. It happened in the second semester of my freshman year at college.

Northeastern University had three semesters each year, while other colleges had only two. I failed the first miserably, which is common with young students who go to college with no real agenda, mostly for something to do after high school, or to please their parents.

My mother was still in tears over the three D's, and the incomplete I managed to get in my physics class, which made my GPA for my first semester a whopping 0.333. I was embarrassed to no end. "Bintell is not college material. He would be better off getting a job. Plus, it would save you a ton of money," is what my father said when he heard my mother crying in the den over my grades. It gets worse.

After watching my mother cry in shame and

embarrassment; and after knowing how much money she was spending to put me through a college she really could not afford, I somehow chose failure. Even though I knew my sister was not going to be able to go to the University of Maryland, the school she desperately wanted to attend because all my mother's money was being spent on me, again, somehow I still chose failure. The question is, why.

For some odd reason, that very next semester, the president and all the professors in the electrical engineering department decided to suddenly change the way things were to be done. Just as I had gotten used to doing things one way, they changed everything because, they felt like it.

The way we took tests, handed in homework, and got our grades were to now be done differently in what they said was the interest of time and energy. Smaller amounts of their time and larger amounts of my energy I am sure. For me, the change was slow and painful. The professors acted as if the entire student body should adjust to this change overnight. Some did. I was not one of them.

To make matters worse, I was taking my first computer class. Fortran was the computer languages name. I will never forget it. I was in a complete state of shock as the teacher wrote our first lesson on the board. It looked like Spanish, and sounded just as unfamiliar. It is one of my least favorite moments in life, but that day, as I watched the professor explain the first line of the computer language, I whispered to myself in a voice so quiet and calm, I can still hear it now. The voice said, "I am not going to pass this class."

And that was it. Just as I said I would, I failed. In spite of Mr. Gullucio, and in spite of my mother's tears and in spite of my strong desire to ease her pain and save her from my father's harsh words. In spite of the fact that I instantly recognized the power in being able to program machines to do what I wanted them to, the pain of dealing with the changes of my school policies, coupled with the pain of figuring out this new language, was just too much. It would subject me to too much physical and emotional discomfort. Not to mention the serious strain on my time and energy that would come from a choice to succeed. I thought failing would be less painful. I was wrong.

> Power is
> the supreme
> control of
> commodities,
> human and
> non-human

Just like Mr. Gullucio told me years prior, "Bintell, you chose those grades the first day you stepped foot in my class," I was doing it again in college. Success, as well as failure, was a conscious choice.

In many a sales meetings, branch managers, VP's of sales and sometimes, even presidents and CEOs always said the same thing. "When Michael Jordan realized he could not dunk on the entire league at will, he developed a fade away jump shot or manufactured points by getting himself to the foul line. Or when Muhammad Ali realized he could not knock his opponents out with pure speed, he adjusted his strategy and invented a style of fighting he called, The Rope-A-Dope, allowing opponents to punch themselves out, wearing them down until they are too tired to stand. You are a sales athlete. Make the necessary adjustment so you can be a success for yourself."

As an adult, I thought once I made the choice to deal with the aches and pains of getting to the office in the morning, my crusade toward success was just a matter of time. Then I got blindsided by all the aches and pains that come from something I had no control over, change.

For people like me, afraid of the pain that came from change, life in the rat race was like being in a horrible street fight. No matter how many times I got knocked down because of my stubbornness and inability to simply change my behavior, I refused to. Like an outdated piece of computer equipment that wouldn't work with the newer cooler model, I stuck to my old ways.

But for other, far more successful people, who made friends with change and learned to manipulate its power, change was just another reason for them to make more and more money.

"EVERYTHING IS IN A PROCESS OF CHANGE, NOTHING ENDURES; WE DO NOT SEEK PERMANENCE."

- MASATOSHI NAITO

SUCCESS = I + C + R

CHANGE IS PROFIT

ॐ

"WHOSOEVER DESIRES CONSTANT SUCCESS, MUST CHANGE HIS
CONDUCT WITH THE TIMES."
- NICCOLO MACHIAVELLI

Life in the rat race was like channel surfing, as change was coming fast and from all angles. There were new managers that wanted things done their way. Some new software package that required hours of my time and energy with data entry. Mergers and acquisitions that in one day made me feel as if my whole life was being turned upside down. Not to mention the changes that were taking place with the customers I was selling my commodities to.

> *"If you want to make enemies, try to change something."*
> Woodrow Wilson

The older salespeople that were quietly making half a million dollars a year advised me to ask the same question to start off every sales meeting. "As soon as you get inside their office, before you sit down, your first question should be, has anything changed since we last met?" Nine times out of 10, the answer was yes. Being blind to changes in sales situations was always a formula for sure failure.

Even when I thought I had done everything perfectly and gotten a customer to agree to buy my commodity, they hesitated, as change was resisted by the company's people tooth and nail. The more I was burned by change, the more I started watching out for it. Change was destroying people inside and outside of the rat race at epidemic proportions.

There were millions upon millions of people trapped in low-income neighborhoods because they would rather die than face the pain of change. Some chose to live in the past as Father Time was handing them too much change to keep up with. Still others would risk heart attacks before changing their diets. Even my favorite commodity, music, was full of colorful "chord changes", making songs emotionally soothing and worth listening to. David Bowie's timeless lyrics made perfect sense. "Turn and face the change...cha-cha-changes..." Then Cheryl Crow followed his lead with a song that went, "The change...will do you good...the change, will do you good... I say the change... will do you good..."

My family members who had come to America to achieve the success they felt was their birthright, refused to change. Like glue, they stuck to the same behavior that had produced failure for them back home. I watched men with families destroy themselves completely as they were too stubborn to change, even in the face of sure failure. Years later, even my mother admitted to me that if she was not willing to change anything, she should have stayed where she was.

My plea to family members that we change our behavior caused nothing short of a riot. They were outraged and felt I was turning my back on what I was. They asked, "What is the matter, we're not good enough for you anymore?"

I replied, "What we are doing is not working. The only difference between us and those people across the road is our bad behavior." Some would shake their heads no and say, "There is nothing that needs to be changed about me. I am as good as I am going to get!" Others would stare at me with tears and pain in their eyes saying not a word. Some would cry and say, "You are supposed to love people and not ask them to change." Their disdain for change in the name of success was scary.

Across the road, the stock market was making people billions, while sending others to the poor house daily, due to the violent daily behavior of change. The world was changing at a constant rate of speed, turning success stories into nightmares, and making dreams come true in the blink of an eye. Those like myself, too afraid of change got run over by it, many times. But the successful people across the road, who were able to stand the ever changing test of time, seemed to make friends with change. While I ran from change as fast as I could, they cleverly used change as a way to make even more money for themselves.

In the rat race, every single person with a commodity was using change as a reason to step on the gas of their genius engine and create yet another hot commodity. Car companies made big cars, then small ones due to changes in gas prices. Clothing designers changed everything each season, inspired by the snow, or the falling leaves, or the rain, or the summer's sunshine. The computer world was in the "change is money" game as well.

Like clockwork, each year, there were changes or what we called, issued upgrades to some small portion of every computer related commodity in sight. Software upgrades so old computers worked with newer models, computers with faster CPU's (Central Processing Units) that processed information faster saving time and energy, new software patches with extended service contracts.

Successful people changed anything and everything about their hot commodities just so they could ask for more money, in the spirit of the new and improved model they called, innovations. While so many were standing still, life was evolving right before my eyes, leaving millions of rigid people like myself in the past. I was stunned by how well the CEOs I was selling products to accepted my sales pitch of change. They would always say, "Yeah, yeah, I know the routine. We do the same thing to our customers." They seemed happy to be buying into the latest and greatest commodities. They even planned for it in their yearly budgets.

If I was working for a company that did not use change as a reason to ask their customers for more money as quickly as their competition, their stock prices would sink, and they would go from the top of the world, to the bottom of the poor house in days, leaving me unemployed and not understanding why.

Employees too set in their ways to change their behavior, were always quickly phased out of the companies I worked for, as the only thing predictable in business, was the unpredictability of how fast things could and would always change. On the other hand, the people who could change on a dime with the times were always the most successful.

Whether they were working for some large multi-billion dollar company, or working for themselves, they were like money making chameleons, as one minute they were making money with this commodity, and in the blink of an eye, they were making money with another.

I listened to my broker friends who had been buying and selling fertilizer for years, talk to associates about how they got wind of the price of fertilizer falling, and how oil's was rising. Then, without warning, they would jump the fertilizer ship and hop on the oil or natural gas bandwagon to keep their success formula spinning.

When famous music producers who had built empires with music exhausted every opportunity to make money, they would re-invent themselves in television, or clothing lines, cleverly using their music as information to sell their latest hot commodities and keep their success formula spinning, while the competitions ran out of gas.

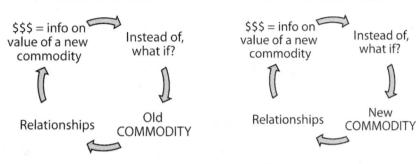

FIRST SUCCESS

$$$ = info on value of a new commodity → Instead of, what if?

↑ Relationships

Old COMMODITY ↓

SECOND SUCCESS

$$$ = info on value of a new commodity → Instead of, what if?

↑ Relationships

New COMMODITY ↓

When I went for a new job, my lack of experience was always the reason why I did, or did not get the job. On the other hand, successful people seemed to care less about experience, as they collected new commodities the way I collected pennies for my piggy bank as a child.

With a successful commodity under their belt, success now chased them. Relationships of all sorts were just waiting at their every beck and call, hopeful to be a part of their newest business endeavor. While others looked on in amazement, stunned by the speed of their meteoric success, they took it all in stride, because what others thought was impossible, they saw as natural. To them, the business of making money was just a game.

Successful people I met and admired who changed effortlessly with the times, always referred to this struggle for money, power and fame as a game. They would say things like, "Step up your game." and, "I've got this game down pat."

At first, the nerve of them to call life's many aches and pains a game offended me. The term seemed arrogant, as I had seen this so called game, wreck havoc in many lives, namely mine. But later, with *The Formula* spinning in my palm, I realized that life, and its many ups and downs, was for a chosen few, a game to be played. For them, money was just a way of keeping score. The question is, how exactly do you play?

CHANGE IS PROFIT

"YOUR SUCCESS IN LIFE IS NOT BASED ON YOUR ABILITY TO SIMPLY
CHANGE. IT IS BASED ON YOUR ABILITY TO CHANGE FASTER THAN
YOUR COMPETITION, CUSTOMERS AND BUSINESS."
- MARK SANBORN

THE BIG GAME

ॐ

"MONEY WAS NEVER A BIG MOTIVATION FOR ME, EXCEPT AS A WAY
TO KEEP SCORE. THE REAL EXCITEMENT IS PLAYING THE GAME."
- DONALD TRUMP- REAL ESTATE BILLIONAIRE

The first time I heard someone casually refer to the pursuit of financial independence as a game, my heart practically skipped a beat. I had only been on the job as a Sales Engineer for a month, yet I found myself on Manhattan's Upper East Side at a party hosted by a dentist for the National Hockey League.

There were successful people of every shape and size imaginable there. Corporate and entertainment lawyers, bankers, actors, record and movie producers, fashion models I am sure I had seen in the pages of Vogue and Elle magazines, visual artist, and one, odd ball Sales Engineer, who clearly did not belong.

I was afforded the luxury of attending this lavish event care of some high school friends who had made better choices than I had in the relationship department while in college. They had strategically acquired fraternal relationships that kept them in touch with the top of New York City's talent pool.

Whenever they threw parties, commodity owners of every shape and size came running, offering them money just to put pictures of their commodities on the dance floor. They soon changed up like a major league pitcher on the mound and transitioned to the world of sales. Three brothers, six Ivy League schools, and three masters degree's later, and they were in the same boat as me. They were salesmen.

They opened an advertising firm which put them in business with some of the largest companies in the world. They were creating marketing and advertising campaigns for large companies who had no idea how to tell people about the pain relief their commodities provided.

In the kitchen we stood, about six of us, listening to this financial wizard talk us through the many details of his financial conquests on Wall Street. With the charisma of an Oscar winning actor delivering an acceptance speech, he explained his game plan to become one of the richest men in the world, right behind Warren Buffett. The models listened to him, hanging off of his every word. He was clearly at the top of his game in more ways than one.

"Most people play the game with one product, while I on the other hand get to play with all of them, or the ones I understand at least. No matter how crazy it looks on the surface, at the end of the day, it's all just a big game," he said as he took a sip of his white wine and unfastened his tie.

"These companies whose stock I buy and sell are all selling the same thing really. I mean, a handful of them have a truly unique product, but most of them are competing with each other. Companies have a few tools available to them to outdo the next guy. At the end of the day, the companies that stick to the fundamentals, always come out on top. The ones that do not, usually get purchased by their competitors. My job is to buy the ones that do, and sell the ones that do not as quickly as possible. If I do this for my clients, I make money, and may I add, lots of money! That's the name of the game for me."

Two of the other guys who had been patiently tolerating his performance left the room. I wanted to do the same but I stayed. I needed to find out what he meant by fundamentals.

"What do you mean fundamentals?" I asked politely.

"Fundamentals meaning basic successful business behavior. All companies have a few fundamental tools at their disposal to craft their success. The first step is having a product millions of people will buy. I mean, without that, nobody wants to play the game and all bets that a product will continue to sell and go up in value are off."

One of the models walked up to him and flirtatiously asked, "Am I a product you think will go up in value?" He took a sip of his wine, smiled at her but said nothing. I jumped in with another question, as if I ever met anyone with a PhD. in Money, it was definitely this guy.

"Is that all there is to it? The fundamentals are just having a product people will buy and you are a mega successful company?"

"No, it takes a bit more than that, and, what are you into?"

"Information technology."

"Okay, I love technology companies. Their products keep changing, so you have to stay on your toes, or you will miss out on a chance to make some real money buying and selling them. Even still, they behave just like any other company. Their marketing and advertising (information that sells) and distribution and sales channels (relationships that sell) are the building blocks to the success of their products. The ones that understand how to use those two things to sell boatloads of their products, (the hot commodity) usually see the value of their stock rise."

His eyes sparkled like a college professor as he went through stories of companies that flooded the market with information on the television, radio, and over the Internet to hypnotize millions into buying a product that was in all reality, no better than the competition.

He told us all about the companies he loved to buy cheap and sell high, full of what he called "strategic relationships". These companies had partnerships of every type imaginable with large distribution channels equipped with national, and even international sales forces. These companies sold tons of their products in months, turning insane profits, and pushing their stock price into the stratosphere, making him millions.

When he talked about companies that were surviving just because they discovered cheaper ways of producing their products, I just knew they got the information to do this from their customers (feedback), the same way my customers gave me great ideas after they used my products.

He made the fundamentals seem like joysticks on a video game. When times changed and people stopped buying things, they simply pushed the handle up or down on one or all of the three success joysticks. They pushed more or less information into the system to convince people to buy, or collected more relationships to help them sell. If they saw that did not work, they dropped the price on their commodities and cut back on relationships by laying people off to make sure no matter what, their success / money machine still spit out the same amount of money. I had to admit, making money and being successful sounded just like playing a video game or adjusting the equalizer on a car stereo.

SUCCESS EQUALIZER

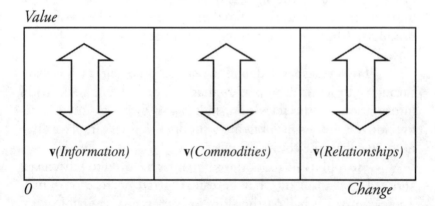

Value

v(*Information*)   **v**(*Commodities*)   **v**(*Relationships*)

0   *Change*

The stock market, the height of wealth, fame and power was all about information to create, and sell commodities, added to strategic relationships, chasing current events or news around and around. This mixture drives stock values up and down, making people billions of dollars every day. The fundamentals this wizard with a PhD in Money was referring to, were actually the individual pieces of *The Formula*.

Success = (Info to create, sell & changes over time) + Commodities + Strategic Relationships = **Billions**

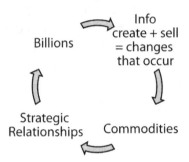

Presidents and CEOs of companies used these three joysticks in times of change to steer their companies through good and bad times. The value of these three tools made their success formulas spin faster, or slower.

Soon the party began to wind down so I left for my train ride back to Long Island. Riding in the cab to 34th Street, staring at the spectacle of wealth and poverty in the New York City streets, I was overcome with guilt and shame as I could not help those in need.

How could regular people compete with the power of worldwide successful companies with money to buy information in big bright lights, engineers who created the best commodities on Earth, and relationships as far as the eye could see? How could I level the playing field for people like myself?

As we drove past the billboards of Times Square on the way downtown to Pennsylvania Station, I saw a picture of one, if not the most recognizable man in all of sports. If nothing else, his life's story is proof that you do not have to be like the guy with the PhD in Money I had just met to play and win in the game of wealth, fame and power.

One of the greatest success stories I have ever heard is one of a man known to the world as The Greatest of All Times. It is a classic tale of success, engineered by a man who was able to use *The Formula* to overcome extreme hatred, while bending the will of the most powerful nation in the world to his agenda.

So let us take a quick break from my journey. Let me take a minute to tell you this timeless story so you can see *The Formula* in action in someone else's life besides mine. This way, there will be no doubt in your mind that *The Formula* does indeed work.

"HAPPINESS IS NOT IN THE MERE POSSESSION OF MONEY; IT LIES IN THE JOY OF ACHIEVEMENT, IN THE THRILL OF CREATIVE EFFORT."

- FRANKLIN D. ROOSEVELT

THE GREATEST OF ALL TIME

&

"MAKE NO MISTAKE MY FRIEND, IT TAKES MORE THAN MONEY TO MAKE MEN RICH."

- A.P. GOUTHEY

If there is any one sports figure who has captured the hearts and minds of the entire world, it would be The Goat, short for the greatest boxer of all time, Mr. Muhammad Ali. To his credit, at the height of his popularity, he was one of the five most recognizable faces on the planet.

Muhammad Ali saw great peaks and valleys in his life. He went from being the most hated person on Earth, to being the most respected and loved sports figure in the world. How he was able to rise from relative obscurity in Louisville, Kentucky, to this coveted place in American and world history, is a story worth taking note of, and a product of *The Formula*.

Muhammad Ali, originally Cassius Clay, was just like any other young man growing up in his day. One sunny day while he was out playing, someone stole his bicycle. In pain over the loss of such a valuable commodity, young Clay, going on feedback from a policeman on the scene, made a choice to take matters of success into his own hands. He immediately enrolled in the local boxing gym. With this choice, a star was born.

Young Ali worked tirelessly in his boxing gym in

Kentucky growing his talent in the sport. He worked so hard, at the 1960 Olympics in Rome; he won three gold medals as a light heavyweight. Back home in the United States, one evening, a friend took him to see a very flamboyant wrestler perform. The wrestlers name was Gorgeous George.

Gorgeous George in his time was said to be just as, if not more recognizable than the President. He was the highest paid athlete of his time and is single-handedly credited with re-inventing the sport of wrestling, giving it national and international attention. Gorgeous George was a flamboyant showman who turned his entry into the ring, into nothing short of a Broadway show.

His performance consisted of him being accompanied by women throwing roses at his feet, another holding a mirror, two others to help him take off his purple cape before each match. He would even spray perfume in the ring and demand the referees wash their hands. People loved to hate him. Hundreds of thousands would pack arenas hoping to see Gorgeous George finally humiliated with a much deserved loss.

As young Ali sat watching the show that so many successful people have modeled their behavior after, such as The King, Elvis Presley, The Godfather of Soul James Brown, The King of Rock and Roll Little Richard, and countless others, he recognized value in showmanship, imagery and personality above and beyond his talent in the sport of boxing. Right then and there, in the name of success, Ali made a choice to reinvent himself.

Success = (Instead of being me, what if I act like Gorgeous George?) + (Cassius Clay) + The World = $$$

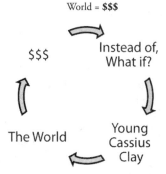

$$$

Instead of, What if?

The World

Young Cassius Clay

In his heavyweight debut, as a serious underdog against the Heavy Weight Champ, the infamous Sonny Liston, Ali taunted Liston in promotional press conferences driving many to believe he was actually insane. He made up jingles predicting the round he would knock Liston out in, which he continued to do throughout his 61 win / 5 loss career. In an upset that in his own words, "Shook up the world!" he beat Liston masterfully. The boxing world was in disbelief and in a subsequent rematch, Ali knocked Liston out seconds into the first round, with a punch he and his trainer invented, which they named "The Phantom Punch."

Ali in his flamboyant Gorgeous George style, told the world that his brand of boxing was, "I fly like a butterfly and sting like a bee." In press conferences being interviewed by the legendary sports commentator Howard Cosell, Ali would rant and rave uncontrollably saying, "I'm pretty Howard! I'm the greatest! I just can't be beat."

You may have loved him, you may have hated him, but come fight night, the world stood at attention, earning this young athlete at the height of his fame and popularity, one of the first million dollar paydays in boxing history. In spite of his incredible success, the young Cassius Clay, in a series of shocking and controversial moves, joined the Nation of Islam, changed his name to Muhammad Ali and for religious reasons, refused to join the Vietnam War draft. In spite of jail time, being stripped of his title and losing his license to box in the USA, Ali stuck to his guns, risking everything he had achieved to that point.

This series of moves caused Muhammad Ali to become the most hated public figure of his time. He lived the next three years in exile. Fortunately, using *The Formula*, he was able to turn this extreme hatred into worldwide love, admiration and success.

Joe Frazier who became the champ as a result of Ali being stripped of his title, in an act of kindness, petitioned President Nixon to get Ali's boxing license reinstated. But instead of being thankful, in true Ali fashion, he took to the airways, taunting Frazier, causing a historic rift between the two men while in the process, drawing so much attention to the fight, it became known as "The Fight of the Century."

Ali used any and all information at his disposal to promote the match. In an ingenious plan, he positioned Joe Frazier as the sellout because he had not opposed the Vietnam War, and himself as the people's champ, playing to the heartstrings of the millions of people in deep emotional pain that felt the Vietnam War was an unjust and inhumane campaign.

The fighters were instantly swept into a media frenzy in various magazine and television stations. Due to the "hype" of the match, they both signed contracts that guaranteed them $2.5 million each, a record payday at that time for a single boxing match.

Success = (Ali Antics + Anti War Sentiment) + (Violence + Ali + Frazier) + (Media + World) =

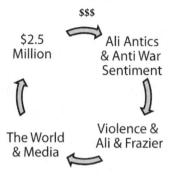

Ali went on to promote other fights in the same fashion. The Thrilla in Manila, being the third fight against Joe Frazier in their long standing feud. The Rumble in the Jungle that took place in Africa's Zimbabwe, where he fought George Forman and won with a style of fighting he invented called The Rope-A-Dope.

Through it all, this personality was able to go from obscurity to fame and fortune, lose it all, and rise to become one of the most celebrated figures in sports throughout the world. He received the Presidential Medal of Freedom on November 9, 2005. In January of 2008 Muhammad Ali was presented with the Presidential Citizens Medal by President George W. Bush. He also received an honorary doctorate of humanities at Princeton University's 260th graduation ceremony. Ali is by boxing enthusiast standards, one of, if not the greatest boxer in the history of the sport.

With all of the ups and downs in his life, as a young boy watching it all play out, it appeared that he was playing a very intense game. As an adult, I'm convinced his life is proof that if you choose to, anyone can use *The Formula* and transform themselves from rags to riches. Using his life as a model for behavior, it proves that making money, as difficult as it may be for some, is really just a game for others. Comparing Ali's life to my humble experiences, I should have realized long ago that

I already knew how to play this game better than I gave myself credit for.

Looking back on an interesting run-in with near death, and an escape from a date with jail time, I realize now, success, social and economic, is indeed just a game. Like Ali needed the right trainer and the media on his team, I too needed the right teammates to earn myself a shot at a world title.

TURNING YOURSELF, OR SOMETHING ELSE, INTO AN INFINITELY VALUABLE COMMODITY, IS REALLY JUST A BIG GAME OF USING THE FORMULA.

ACT SEVEN

Success = Information + Commodities + Relationships = \$\$\$

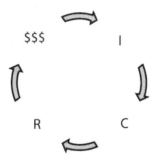

GOLD MINE

SUCCESS = I + C + R

SAVED BY THE COMMODITY

&

PEOPLE LOOK UP TO AND WORSHIP THOSE THAT OWN OR CAN
CREATE COMMODITIES OF GREAT VALUE.

My mother always said, "Any talent that you have, it is your duty to pass it along to your children, so they can use it to protect themselves from life's many ups and downs." No truer words have ever been spoken. I learned the value of these wise words the hard way in high school.

For kids like me, whose family was always moving from place to place like nomads, in addition to being the skinniest kid on my block, constantly bullied by the older, stronger guys in my South Shore neighborhood, a healthy social life was like finding a needle in a hay stack. In my eyes, a commodity more valuable than even money, success if you will, was the happiness and power of friendships, better known as popularity.

When we made our final move from the South Shore to the North Shore, many days I would sit and bellyache to my mother about having no friends as she sewed clothes for my sister and I. I was lost in a sea of unfamiliar faces in our new middle-class neighborhood, but still, not about to give up on my dream of a healthy social life. Maybe if I was lucky, popularity wasn't out of reach.

145

One day I came up with a game plan to turn my social life around. Excited, I sat and shared part of my plan with Mom. The conversation was a long emotional one, as it seemed that she too had similar aspirations of popularity in her younger days.

With a gleam in her eye, she told me about a dress she made one summer which caused the entire neighborhood of girls to show up at her doorstep, begging to borrow it. How they promised to have it cleaned properly before they brought it back she bragged.

"Truthfully, I was shocked they got up the nerve to ask me for it, as most of them had never so much as sneezed my way before my sacred dress came on the scene. That dress made me a superstar," she said as she laughed and shook her head from side to side. Mom explained how after that, she began sewing regularly, making most of her clothes, and in time developing a bit of talent on her sewing machine. Watching her sew every day, I learned how to stitch a hem or two in my pants as well.

As my first full week passed in my new North Shore neighborhood with no sign of massive social acceptance in sight, my desperation to achieve the popularity that had evaded me all my life began to boil over. Frustrated, I moved forward with my plan to sell myself in a package deal with the one commodity I was sure everyone on the South Shore would buy----violence. Like a scene straight from Guys and Dolls in my 6th grade play, I planned to reinvent myself as the new neighborhood tough guy.

SUCCESS = I + C + R

Success = Game Plan + (Violence & ME) + Admirers = **Popularity**

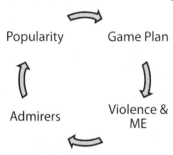

Popularity   Game Plan

Admirers   Violence & ME

On the South Shore, because most people had little or no use for information other than when it was being used to sell them a commodity in an entertaining television commercial, or when they had to memorize just enough of it to take a test for a job, creating a commodity was an unusual occurrence. On the South Shore, hard labor or violence was used to acquire commodities people believed might have the smallest amount of value. The people looking on from the North Shore called this violence senseless.

Commodities like respect, money, or anything else that people felt might have value was acquired on the South Shore not with information to create it, but with either painful backbreaking hard labor, or the deadly threat of violence to take it by force.

Because of this lack of appreciation for information on the South Shore, the gangs, thugs and hooligans lived and died by the violent models of behavior they saw displayed before them and on television. Successful businessmen far removed from the violence of South Shore neighborhoods recognizing violence was a hot commodity, packaged it as a product for the violent hungry people of the world to purchase.

South Side Violence

$$$ → Threat of Violence or Hard Labor

Buyers ← Commodities

Corporations Selling Violence

$$$ → Info

Public ← Violence

People in my new North Shore neighborhood did not spend most of their time fertilizing their talent in violence with repetition. Instead, they were more interested in which college they would attend, and where they were going for summer vacations. Because of this, I thought for sure they would admire my rare brand of violence. Little did I know, there was a group of young men, just across the road, well equipped to outsell me with a very serious brand of violence of their own. They called themselves, The Untouchables.

I rode into school the following Monday with my game plan in full swing. Straight leg pants on girls and guys had come in style due in large part to MTV and music videos starring artists like Madonna and Prince. Because my mother had given me free reign on her sewing machine, I was able to alter my pants with great precision, putting myself right on the cutting edge of popular culture and fashion.

As I walked through the halls of my new school, a vision of popular culture in my fashion forward outfit, I made sure to notify as many people as possible about how much of a tough guy I was. This information packaged with my altered clothing exploded all over school grounds.

As I hoped, the news spread around town like wildfire about the "new tough guy" in town. Before I knew it, everyone wanted to know who I was, and even more importantly, The

Untouchables put a bounty on my head. Although dangerous, the plan was working. I was finally popular.

As sophomore year approached, my popularity grew. But my success was overshadowed with the serious threat of doom. The Untouchables were growing more impatient, as they wanted me eliminated once and for all. I was briefed by my loyal followers on the credentials of each one of them. All were pretty tough, but one of them stood out as the toughest.

His name was Benjamin Rogers. He was a golden glove boxer who had made short work of the strongest, most menacing characters in town. One day he came walking into the school lobby and calmly sat down. I watched him in awe from behind the lunchroom window. I feared and admired him at the same time.

Later that week, the worst thing happened. The Untouchables caught me walking home by myself. Twenty of them surrounded me. A short, stocky character who looked like a running back for a college football team approached me. He stepped right in front of me and before I could say a word, he slapped me across the face.

I was stunned and angered by his nerve. I wanted to defend myself, but the thought of 20 menacing Untouchables stopped me from reacting. I looked around, and all 19 of his Untouchable friends, as they stood there watching the show. Somehow, my eyes looked directly into Ben's. Before I could think, another stinging slap raked across my face.

The pressure was mounting. I needed to make a choice. They were both bleak. My pride and reputation were on the line on one hand, but if I fought back, extreme pain was the inevitable. What should I do? Another slap, and then another. I looked at the overdeveloped guy in front of me wearing clothes fit for a homeless person, and just as his hand began to wind up for another go round, Ben stepped in.

"That's enough. This is me talking now. Don't hit him again!" Not one word was uttered after that. All 19 of them turned around and walked up the block. Ben looked at me and said, "You alright?" I said nothing. Too ashamed of what had happened, I could not even look into his eyes. Then out of nowhere he said, "Hey, I like the pants. Can you fix mine? I heard you fix yours on your mother's sewing machine." Ben and I are to this day the best of friends.

I fixed Ben's pants and he gave me just enough boxing lessons to protect myself from The Untouchables. I happily purchased his commodity, and he purchased mine. Ben thought it was an even trade, but it wasn't. He paid me twice, as he told everyone who was responsible for altering his favorite jeans.

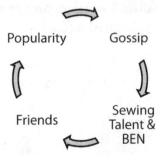

Ironically, I now had supreme control over the entire town, exactly what I wanted from the very start. The success I stumbled upon overshadowed the embarrassment of being flogged by one of The Untouchable's finest. My relationship with the toughest guy in the neighborhood, coupled with my desired sewing commodity, caused such gossip throughout the town, it made me popular and, powerful.

Soon the entire neighborhood was at my door. People brought me nine, sometimes 10 pairs of pants at a time. They offered me anything of value, including money. It was just like my mother had described. I was a superstar.

Before I knew it, my mother's sewing machine was buried under a pile of pants in need of my famous alterations. I charged $6 a pair for the pleasure of owning the look Ben had popularized for me. Although I later ran for most popular and lost, I managed to somehow shrug it off. I had come a long way.

> *The service industry makes up for more than 60% of the United States Economy. It is worth $8.5 trillion*

Years later, I watched famous clothing designers worth millions and billions of dollars use actors, actresses, musicians and models the same way I used Ben in high school. I just smiled as I obviously was not the only one who had successfully played this clothing game on the public at large.

I thought my days of playing games with commodities and escaping near death were long gone, but a few years later, I managed to get myself into another tight situation. Commodities rescued me again, this time, springing me from jail better than any lawyer ever could have.

WHEN PEOPLE DO NOT HAVE MONEY TO PURCHASE NEW COMMODITIES, THEY CAN FALL INTO STATES OF DEPRESSION AS THE ACT OF SHOPPING RELEASES CHEMICALS IN THE BODY THAT RELAX AND SEDATE. THE CHEMICALS ARE SIMILAR TO THE ONES RELEASED WHEN PEOPLE EAT FOOD. IT IS KNOWN AS RETAIL THERAPY. NATIONAL ECONOMIES BEHAVE THE SAME WAY. WHEN ITS PEOPLE CANNOT BUY NEW COMMODITIES, THE COUNTRY WILL FALL INTO A RECESSION AND EVEN WORSE, AN ECONOMIC DEPRESSION.

JAIL BREAK

&

EVERY RELATIONSHIP YOU HAVE, OR WILL EVER HAVE, IS A REACTION TO A VALUABLE COMMODITY YOU POSSESS. THIS COMMODITY MAY BE YOU.

A few years passed and I happily settled into the non-violent social norms of my North Shore town. Because we were living on the edge of one of the wealthiest neighborhoods in America, the police were seldom seen. As a result, I paid no attention to them. I neglected a court date for a period of two years while I was away at college. Certainly, they would understand. I had no time for tickets and court while working so hard to graduate.

One day on summer break, my mother approached me in the den while I was practicing my guitar. "Bintell, you have a court date and I cannot help you this time. I have been here paying ticket after ticket for you with money I do not have trying to keep your license clean. This you will have to do on your own. Do not miss this court date Bintell." I decided to go to court, as I was sure I could talk my way out of just about any situation.

I got to court and the atmosphere was as tense as my run in with The Untouchables. The judge, a little grey haired man who wore his glasses on the tip of his nose was all business. "Guilty…see the clerk…guilty…pay the cashier…guilty!" was his battle cry. I feared for the worst.

"Mr. Powell?" I approached the bench slowly.

"Yes?"

He looked through my file and asked, "Why haven't you been able to make your court dates for the past two plus years may I ask?"

"Well sir, I was away in college and I never received any of these letters."

"For two, almost three years Son? Not one letter? We have sent a total of 15 letters to your residence. You do live at 835 Eastfield Road?"

"Yes sir, I do." Two court officers moved in behind me slowly. I turned and looked at the one standing to my right in disbelief. Were they going to arrest me?

"Son, because you won't appear in court, I have to remand you," he said as the officers grabbed me from the back and put the handcuffs on me. I was in shock. Me? I was being arrested? I was escorted into the back like a common criminal. My mother was going to kill me for sure.

They brought me in the holding room and it hit me, I was going to jail. The place I just knew I would never ever have to go. I had taken things too far and now, my mother was going to have to tell her friends the apple of her eye, her son, who she spent her last dollar to make an engineer, was in jail.

I saw other young men, who had obviously made just as poor choices as me, dressed in orange jump suits being escorted to a bus just outside the holding area. I put myself mentally in a place I had not gone in years. I replayed the days of The Untouchables and prepared to meet the potential for violence, with a very serious brand of violence of my own.

The policeman came to my cell and waved me to follow him. He said, "Please take off all metal objects and put them in the tray." I began surrendering all my most valuable possessions. My keys, wallet, necklace, and the most valuable commodity on my person, the Rolex watch I purchased with left over tuition money my mother had no idea about.

The officer looked through everything but when he picked up the watch, he stopped, looked up at me and said, "Is this a real Rolex?"

"Yes," I responded sensing a weird kindness in his eyes. We stared at each other for about five seconds, saying not a word. His next words were unexpected. He said, "You do not belong here. Go call your parents. Tell them your bail is $500. Hurry up. Get yourself out of here."

In less than an hour, I was escorted out the back door where my mother and my sister were waiting. Mom gave me an earful, but when I said, "Mom, you are right. I always let things go until the last minute. I have got to be more responsible." She calmed down, for at least a minute or two.

As I rode home, I polished my watch with pride. My mother kept screaming, but I was calm as a cucumber. In the middle of her giving me the tongue lashing of my life, I said, "Mom, do you remember when I said that everything good, I mean really good that has happened to me socially, has been a result of something I owned that I had no business having; something really expensive?" Confused, she looked at my sister and then she scowled at me as if she wanted to have my head examined. I felt very important in light of what had happened, so I kept on talking.

"Like when I was invited to that mansion party in Connecticut with those rich twins only because you let me use your Audi as if it was mine last summer?" We pulled to a red light and she turned around slowly, looking deep into my eyes to see if I had gone completely mad.

"Have you lost your mind completely?" she asked. "Do not think for a minute I am going to pay that $500 bail. You are paying me back if it takes the rest of your life. And, I am telling your father!" I looked down at the small, valuable piece of jewelry wrapped around my wrist with pride.

"Mom, sometimes the things you own can save your life."

From that moment on, I was hooked on high priced commodities, turning my nose up at anything that was not a status symbol, as I felt it would not give me power over people. The more expensive it was the better. Paying a lot of money for something was far less painful than the emotional pain of being a social misfit or even worse, the physical and emotional pain of jail time.

Once I got into the rat race and started making more money than my young eyes had ever seen, like millions of people throughout the world, trying to sell themselves to the already successful people they admire, I did what I always do. I took it much too far.

60% OF THE COMMODITIES PRODUCED AROUND THE WORLD ARE CONSUMED IN THE UNITED STATES.

ADDICTED

&

"I DO NOT DESIGN CLOTHES, I DESIGN DREAMS."
- RALPH LAUREN

The thrill of those first $30,000 commission checks earned as a Sales Engineer for Canon USA was a big boost for my young, impressionable sales ego. Although the much needed success was due completely to all three parts of *The Formula* working together, I foolishly convinced myself that me closing deals with ease had a lot to do with all my overpriced symbols of status.

It was almost impossible not to lust for high prices status symbols. In New York City, every free space of every wall on every street was littered with information to sell something. Like an economy when people do not spend money on things, I had to buy something to keep myself from falling into a serious depression. To avoid the emotional pain of being a social misfit, I bought everything I could, and could not afford.

Selling myself with the least amount of risk for bodily harm was my goal, so I turned my back on the obvious power of violence being sold on television. Instead, designer clothing, duplex apartments and exotic cars of all shapes and sizes were the tools of my sales trade.

To get my success formula to spin far enough around to attract the most powerful relationships New York had to offer, I purchased the right watch, so other successful people would trust my time was valuable. I found a comfortable lane in the right Range Rover, wore the right designer suit, equipped with $100 ties and $100 pocket squares. I could not make enough money fast enough to fulfill all of my commodity desires.

Success = (Info. from status symbols to sell me) + (ME & Status Symbols) + (Powerful Friends) =

(Social Acceptance & Missing Money Machine Pieces)

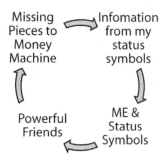

This game plan worked perfectly. Well, almost. When I was out on the town, I did not have to say a word as my high-priced status symbols did the talking for me. In fact, they worked better when I kept my mouth closed, as they spoke a potent success language my words could never compete with.

Invitations to the best social gatherings New York had to offer found their way into my email inbox. I was in the "in crowd" and "in style," and finally as popular as I ever wanted to be. But I soon learned that when you blindly buy expensive things, in time, they have a way of owning you.

I was not a rich celebrity, so my fancy social life was tied to a relationship with a friend, which made socializing feel just like being a Sales Engineer. My social sales partner's name was Jason.

Jason owned a small advertising firm he built from scratch. I used my high priced commodities to sell myself to Jason, and in turn, he helped me sell myself to the CEOs of New York City's social scene at night.

Jason dropped out of Boston University's Business Administration program in his second year and started his advertising company with sheer determination and a squeaky clean corporate image. Over a 10 year period, I watched Jason build his company one valuable relationship at a time.

Jason sold his talents for designing advertising campaigns for large companies to help them sell their commodities to people like, himself. He collected long term relationships with companies like Coca Cola, Motorola, The US Army, CVS and various popular musicians. These multi-billion dollar companies hired him because they knew Jason knew exactly how to get their commodity in good with a very powerful sales partner, popular culture. They trusted him with the success of their commodities as Jason was not just another salesman, Jason was popular culture in the flesh.

Jason knew the aches and pains of the working class better than they knew themselves. He also knew just about everyone in New York's party scene on a first name basis and like me, he used expensive status symbols as a means of getting close enough to anybody, to sell them just about anything.

As a team, Jason and I used our high priced commodities to gain entry to the most exclusive social events New York had to offer. Fashion shows filled with celebrities that lined the edge of the catwalks like jewelry, making it hard to concentrate on the clothes being showcased, summer parties in the Hamptons, and exclusive five-star restaurants were our playgrounds.

Every single one of the successful people we hung out with in all these upscale places were either salespeople for some powerful Fortune 500 company, or ex-salespeople turned CEOs, now selling themselves and a product they owned in a package deal. The ones that were still working for Fortune 500 companies were "pay for performance" employees, paid on the amount of money they were able to generate for their company. They were just like Jason and I. They were salespeople.

Jason's advertising company exploded as he was socializing with the very people he was trying to do business with. On the other hand, my world as a salesman crumbled every six months, as the people buying computers from me during the day, were not in upscale bars and restaurants at night. Luckily, there was always unemployment to keep my head above water. And with my expensive clothes, status symbols and Jason as a teammate, socially, I did not miss a beat.

The excitement of using my high priced status symbols like a magnet to attract so many successful people to me was intoxicating. Once I was in their circle, I was amazed by how simple the commodities that made them successful were. Some sold a service like cleaning offices, while others were selling things as simple as paperclips and hangers.

The simplest of commodities which I took completely for granted, made these people incredible amounts of money, putting their money machines into high gear. Their commodities may not have been as complex as the computer systems I was designing during the day were, but they relieved pain and produced lots of money just the same.

Convinced I was getting close to my own success, by if nothing else association, I ran around town like a madman hoping that someplace along the line, someone would let me in on that big success ingredient I was missing so I could finally complete the design of my money machine.

My bad commodity behavior got worse and worse with each new relationship. But time, after time, after time, it happened. Just as I got close enough to these successful people; close enough for them to tell me all their success secrets, my relationship with them would evaporate into thin air.

Excited about being in the midst of the people with their high-speed money machines already built, never once did I stop and ask myself, "Are these relationships dying because my money machine is not as fast as theirs?" I shied away from the failure of losing these relationships, and embraced the success of attracting new ones.

Buying expensive things put my lonely heart at ease, releasing relaxing endorphins in my body, as I knew people would be magnetically attracted to my high priced things. I functioned better when I was sure my social life was intact. The sense of inclusion I got from these fleeting relationships was calming. They actually made me feel like I was a better person.

In research for this book, I learned that loneliness is a condition that can cause heart disease, affect the immune system, and cause serious depression. Others believe a weak social life can even cause early death. Studies show that loneliness in young people causes them to drop out of school and even resort to delinquency.

My addiction to high priced "things" was as serious as any chemical dependency. I was a shopaholic. Then, just as I was about to buy myself off the side of a cliff, Jason had a revelation that woke me up to the reality that my money machine was not working properly because it was missing the most important piece. I was embarrassed I had not figured it out sooner quite frankly. Being an engineer, it should have been more than obvious to me.

PEOPLE ARE ATTRACTED TO AND CHASE AFTER VALUABLE COMMODITIES ONLY. THIS IS THE TRUE MEANING OF THE LAW OF ATTRACTION.

PRIMARY & SECONDARY

❧

"I AM NOT A DRIVEN BUSINESSMAN, BUT A DRIVEN ARTIST. I NEVER THINK ABOUT MONEY. BEAUTIFUL THINGS MAKE MONEY."
- GEOFFREY BEENE

One summer while Jason and I were at the peak of our posturing and imagery, we both got hit by a good dose of failure that snapped us back into reality. I had just lost yet another sales job, and Jason, unlike himself, lost a multi-million dollar advertising deal to a competing company. The reason for both of our failures was a common culprit in the game of wealth, fame and power---relationships.

The company I was working for hired me to do two things. Within a six-month period, develop relationships with 10 presidents of Fortune 500 companies. Then, in the following six months, I had to use those same relationships to sell $3 million worth of computers. Unfortunately for me, every company I called had already been contacted by this older salesman on my team.

When I made a call to a president or a CEO, I heard the same thing. "We are already dealing with a gentleman from your company." He was a very mild mannered individual, the complete opposite of the typical aggressive salesman personality.

He could afford to be mild mannered and calm because he had relationships with the most powerful consultants and partners New York City had to offer.

He consistently outsold the entire team and was rumored to have made close to two million dollars every year for the past seven years working from home. His antics were just like mine when I was working for Canon USA as a Sales Engineer, only he did not abuse his money machine. The people in the office that did not know how many partners he had working with and for him called him a sales-magician.

The president of the company adored him. They vacationed together care of the company's private yacht. My manager did every, and anything to keep him happy, as the last thing they needed was him to leave and take his priceless relationships to the competition.

It was my sixth month on the job and I had not sold a half a million dollars worth of candles, much less computers. Although I felt I was being set up to fail by my own team member, the next month I was let go for what they called, a lack of performance.

Jason on the other hand lost his multi-million dollar advertising deal to a firm with a partner so powerful, it could sell tons of the company's products he was competing for in the blink of an eye. Like Jason and I had been doing for years, the competition used a flashy commodity to solidify most of their deals. The commodity they used to steal this deal has, and will continue to be used like a formula to sell everything and anything under the sun. The commodity happened to be one of my personal favorites----music.

Their CEO was an ex record executive who had produced music for artists of every genre, but in time, left to pursue his true passion, sales by way of marketing and advertising. With long-standing relationships from his days in the music business, and an understanding of how music is used to sell just about anything, this cunning salesman was designing advertising campaigns full of catchy jingles sung by trustworthy pop stars, to sell everything from lipstick, to jewelry, to bubble gum.

I used to hang out in Jason's office to pass the time in between meetings. This day after he received word of losing his big deal, he got on his soapbox and gave the entire office an earful.

"Working to help these companies sell their products is a way to make a living, but if we are ever going to make real money, we need to own the product we are selling!"

It was such an obvious fact it was invisible. I was stunned by the simple truth of it. So stunned, I had to take a minute to let his words sink in. With all I had discovered just a few years ago about genius and passion, plus me being the engineer and all, you would have thought those words would have been coming out of my mouth.

"Look at all the money we're spending on our image. This expensive office space, our high-priced publicist, designer clothes, linen cards with sterling silver engraved card cases, that $100,000 Range Rover I show up in at special events, dinners wining and dining clients, limousines and so on. We know how to make people buy just about anything. We create the imagery that sells everyone else's stuff. If we owned the product, we could take all these flashy things and use them to sell our stuff. As it stands now, these things are liabilities. They cost us more than they make us. But if we had our own products, they would become instant assets, as they would help us sell just about anything."

The good news is, once I wrote my first book, I was able to turn the tables on the formula that had made such a fool of me for years. Selling it door to door, I turned my high-priced liabilities into assets, as they helped push my book sales through the roof in the New York City area.

But how could I have been so blind? How did I allow my ego to let my social agenda get so far out of whack? Where did I learn that my image was the only thing I could use to convince society I was a valuable commodity? Was it because I had moved around all my life and desperately needed friends? Was I modeling myself after the celebrities who were worshiped like gods on television and in magazines for their excessively priced status symbols? Or maybe it was that first taste of popularity and success in high school? Could that near brush with jail have been the turning point? In the ultra materialistic streets of New York City, on any given day it's obvious, Jason and I were far from alone in our image addiction.

But, even if I was not alone in my bad behavior, I was still ashamed of myself as I quietly sat and listened to Jason's big speech. I willingly bought myself a one way ticket to economic failure desperately seeking social success. Did I think I was not smart enough to create a product? Was I afraid to think?

I like so many others had chosen failure, too afraid of standing on my own two feet and doing my part to protect the world from pain by creating something. I took the easy way out, confusing success and popularity by way of only buying things, with true financial success by way of creating and selling--things. Or maybe the two were somehow connected?

The more I asked these tough questions, the more I realized how instinctual my misguided behavior actually was. A natural urge to be socially accepted using a simple formula for success to sell myself to the world at large. On a basic level, everyone was buying things not just to ease their pain, but also to commoditize and sell themselves to their peers.

The formula is, "value by association" with other valuable commodities. I was commoditizing myself by wrapping myself in as many other valuable commodities as possible, hoping society would first look at the commodities, and then look at me and see success. But, as Jason pointed out, we were both missing one major piece of our money machine in our quest for success.

There were primary as well as secondary commodities. In the case of our outlandish antics, our image was our primary commodity. We were using it to replace information to get our success formula to spin. The problem was, we had no secondary commodity to sell along with our primary one in a package deal. We were running PONZI schemes as we were seeking financial success with an empty money machine. Well, we had the commodities of the people we were working for, and this is why we were only partially successful, compared to the ultra successful people in New York City we were trying desperately to model ourselves after.

Michael Jordan's athletic image sells Nikes. Martha Stewart's wholesome image sells everything from pots and pans to candles. Donald Trump is using his image as a supreme businessman, with the help of his reality show to keep his brand trustworthy. Singers like Britney Spears or Jessica Simpson have lifestyle brands and use the imagery in their videos and music to help keep their clothing, swimwear and perfume lines alive and trustworthy.

When the money settles in the bank account of these social icons, people have purchased a piece of that person. Britney Spears herself said it best in one of her songs, "You want a piece of me…" To take risk out of their money machines design, many of these successful people hired image consultants.

Success = (Image / Primary) + Secondary Commodity + Buyers = **$$$**

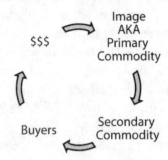

To super-charge their money machines, they add public relations specialists, clothing stylists, hair stylists, and so on. I thought my image was costing me a pretty penny, but theirs was costing them a small fortune. Their behavior was driving the entire luxury industry in America and abroad. Like many people, I believed that if I had the things they had, maybe our lives were somewhat comparable. On some levels it was, but my money machine was missing parts.

They had a primary commodity being their image, and a secondary commodity being their music, clothes, and so on, they were selling the world in a package deal. Jason and I did not. They'd been using this primary / secondary commodity routine on Jason, myself, and the world at large to get their money machines to spit out tons of money for years. When I tried to model myself after these people without having a secondary commodity of my own to sell, I just purchased myself closer and closer to the poor house.

A young man I grew up with came to mind once I saw my mistake. He did the exact opposite of what Jason and I had done. He used information and relationships to become the supreme ruler of all commodities—a president / CEO. Watching his behavior was like watching a clinic or a "How to Class" on becoming the president of a company.

Had I paid just as much attention to information and relationships as I did my image and other people's high priced commodities, maybe I could have become president of one of the many companies I had worked for? I would have been the one to set the speed and pace for the rat race, instead of the mouse on a spinning wheel, trying desperately to keep up with it.

YOU CAN TURN LIABILITIES INTO ASSETS WHEN YOU HAVE ANOTHER COMMODITY TO SELL WITH THEM IN A PACKAGE DEAL.

ACT EIGHT

Success = Information + Commodities + Relationships = $$$

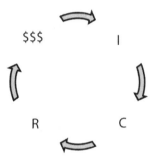

GAME
CHANGER

ACE IN THE HOLE

&

There are a few things that stick out in my mind as life changing experiences. That special Christmas morning of my younger days. The first time I hit the ball in a Little League baseball game. My first kiss. All of these experiences I cherish dearly, as they changed and shaped my view of the world instantly and forever. For me, that list would be incomplete if I did not include my first real run in with the power of organized relationships.

I was finally graduating. Pride in this monumental accomplishment seemed to transform me. I walked upright and with a new sense of pride and confidence. All I had left to do was take one last final exam. One more test and the world of wealth, fame and power would soon be mine for the taking.

I somehow managed to get through the three page formulas of the other five exams alive, but this one class was truly a killer. It was a class I had put off for my entire college career thinking if nothing else, it would be an easy A. I was wrong.

This class and the professor were out for blood. The class was titled, Midler Year Writing Requirement. Realizing this class was going to be anything but easy, I decided to organize a study group to share information and come out on top.

The final exam was a 50-paged paper on a choice of 10 topics chosen by the professor. Designing the paper so it made sense was not as easy as it sounded. The professor was intent on showing us not one ounce of mercy. It soon became apparent that writing was going to be just as, if not more difficult than designing a computer from scratch. On top of that, organizing my fellow classmates into a study group proved to be 10 times harder than anything I had ever done.

The people I tried to bring together seemed intent on doing their papers on their own. I would call them in the morning and set up a meeting place. They would agree, but when I got to the meeting place in the library, the only person there was the person with the least amount of information next to myself.

Sensing my study group was not going to come together, I decided to begin writing two weeks before the due date. I wrote the paper 10 times and then when I thought it was ready, I re-wrote it 10 times more. The day before the final exam, I was confident my paper was finally ready to hand in.

Most of my professors throughout my college career would always advise, "Make sure you have a good breakfast before each exam." Brain food is what they called it. Even though all I had to do was drop my paper off, I decided to have a power breakfast anyway. One hour before the last test of my college career, I went to the famous school diner on Huntington Avenue to eat this ceremonial breakfast, alone.

The large diner looked like an empty church. I sat down close to a window, ordered my omelet, orange juice and toast with butter, then opened my paper to read it through for errors one last time. Before I could take a bite of my toast, it happened.

The door of the diner flew open and 75 students filed into the diner like a football team entering the field for the Super Bowl.

They sat down and began chattering at each other, pointing at notebooks, passing notes between each other as they ate their food. They were all in the same class. They were shouting to each other across the room from different tables. Incredible jealously got the better of me watching this 75 person study group in action.

I could not believe what I was witnessing. At first I thought it was some prank or worse, a bad dream, but it was real. They were all dressed in black designer clothing and they spoke a foreign language. I did not understand a word they were saying but what was clear was, they were working together with the precision of a colony of army ants. Then, as suddenly as they entered the diner, they vanished.

They did not even ask the waiter for the bill. They just threw money on the table and got up and walked out. I sat there shocked. Too stunned to eat my food, feeling lonely and vulnerable, I paid my bill, walked out and made my way to my professor's office.

I dropped the paper in the slot of her office door still in a daze from what I had just witnessed. Then, to clear my head for the last time, I went to the gym.

Working out alone, in the cold gym listening to the weights clank against each other was an eerie experience. It was almost a sign of what would come later once I was firmly inside the rat race. An hour and a half later leaving the gym, they appeared again. This time they were giving each other high fives and hugging. I assumed they did well.

Back in New York, aware of the value of a collective effort, I compared the behavior of people on the North Shore to those on the South Shore relative to the power of the relationships they nurtured. The lack of social and financial success on the South Shore now made perfect sense.

On the South Shore of Long Island, not only did we overlook the value of information, we overlooked the value of relationships as well. The strategic ones I watched the leaders of the rat race use to make millions of dollars were taken for granted almost completely on the South Shore. The people on the North Shore did the exact opposite.

They were so excited about relationships, they had parties to celebrate them called networking events, where they drank, laughed and exchanged business cards, overjoyed by the simple fact that, they had each other. On the South Shore, we were not half as excited about each other. We had an appreciation for those relationships most people usually stumble upon in everyday life. They were:

1. Family
2. Friends
3. Romantic
4. Employee to Employer
5. Organized Gangs

The people on the North Shore were pretty much the same, but there was one major difference between the two ways of life.

On the North Shore, people loved their friends and family members dearly. They had employee to employer relationships, even though most times, they were the employer. They had romantic relationships that usually led to marriage, and the close friends they made in church or through the sporting events of their children. These relationships were just as important to them as they were to the people on the South Shore. The big difference was in the organized relationships that were not just social, but economic as well. On the South Shore, these relationships were practically non-existent.

The people on the North Shore danced around one another holding hands, celebrating their collective success with associations, clubs, councils and members of the board. The people on the South Shore, ashamed of their lack of individual success, were barely able to say good morning to each other on a daily basis.

They hid from each other, hoping to keep their failure a secret. They were so secretive and resentful of one another for the success they did not have, they barely looked each other in the eye, much less said hello, even when they desperately needed help. The mantra on the South Shore seemed to be, "Every man for himself."

As a result of this go it alone mentality, they held tight to their jobs, entrusting all the hopes and dreams of success for themselves and their families, in a paycheck, limited health benefits and two-week vacations each year.

While the parents on the South Shore were off laboring for just enough money to get them home and back to work the next day, the youth on the South Shore, watching their parents being beaten up by the rat race with no end in sight, made obvious, yet dangerous choices in the relationship department. Dangerous as their choices were, they understood that what they needed most, was help.

Searching for popularity, power, and help squaring off against the $14 trillion money machine they lived in called the United States, these children joined forces with the only powerful organizations they felt could lend them a helping hand---gangs.

I AM BECAUSE YOU ARE... WE NEED EACH OTHER TO BE.

THE FORMULA

GANGRENE

&

POWER IS THE SUPREME CONTROL OF COMMODITIES, HUMAN AND
NON-HUMAN.

Like all organized relationships, these gangs were out for one thing, power. The kind of power that comes from supreme control of those commodities desired by many. Other than hard labor, the most reliable commodities people on the South Shore believe they had access to, was the violence they used to acquire commodities by force. As a result, manpower was always very important to these gangs. The more manpower, the more violence they could impose to acquire more and more commodities, money and power.

These gangs recruited just as aggressively as the recruiters that found me a new job every six months. The interview and hiring process for these gangs was brutal. The more powerful the gang, the higher the cost to join. Sometimes, the cost of entry was the most valuable commodity of all, a human life.

On the other hand, the interview process for the gangs on the North Shore was not so much physically brutal, as they were emotionally and mentally taxing. While the gangs on the South Shore made a point of informing their potential employees of their brand of violence, the North Shore gangs were very secretive about their proceedings.

The North Shore gangs were only interested in those who had proven themselves to be information processing, pain resistant machines. The South Shore gangs recruited candidates that could inflict pain, while the North Shore gangs recruited candidates that could endure pain.

Those special few pain resistant people were handpicked and made offers they just could not refuse by the North Shore gangs. Upon entry, relationships powerful enough to hand you just about anything you wanted, embraced you with open arms. I watched one of these North Shore "gangs" turn a friend of mine into the CEO of a major entertainment company, right before my very eyes.

My first day in high school on the North Shore, I met the most popular guys in the neighborhood, the Erickson twins. While walking through the halls of my new school, staring into the eyes of so many new faces, I asked the older twin for a dime to use the pay phone. He was nice enough to oblige, and that is where our friendship began.

There were three brothers in total. A set of twins and an older brother by about a year named Mark. Although I ended up running for most popular two years later, it was the twins that everyone loved and adored. To this day, I have never seen kids so young, yet so aware of the power of relationships.

Years after his rise to power, the oldest brother Mark admitted to me as if he was telling an incredible secret, how he learned the value of strategic relationships watching his father use them to provide the Erickson family, as well as our entire neighborhood, with a small piece of the American Dream.

Mr. Erickson was the neighborhood therapist. The few times I came to visit them while the family was having dinner, their father would be talking to them as if they were sales managers in a quarterly meeting being brought up to speed on a Go-To-Market strategy for some new product.

When young men like the Untouchables got out of hand, the courts would recommend they see Mr. Erickson for psychological treatment, in a last ditched attempt to avoid jail time. This relationship between the criminal justice system and Mr. Erickson provided their family with the largest house in our neighborhood, fully loaded, equipped with every modern day commodity of comfort.

Their older brother was a strange, yet charismatic individual. He marched to the beat of his own drum. It was as if he had a plan to control the world, while the rest of us just wanted to watch music videos on MTV all day. Although he was different, we all looked up to him. He was like E.F. Hutton. When Mark spoke, everyone listened.

On the North Shore, it was expected that everyone would go to college, while on the South Shore, a good job after graduation from high school was the way. When word got back to us through the twins that Mark would be attending Yale for undergraduate studies as well as pledging a national fraternity, everyone decided to do the same. While Mark was away at school, we kept tabs on his social and academic maneuverings care of his brothers on a weekly, sometimes daily basis. When he became part of a fraternity, it was like we were all in the fraternity.

While gangs like the Untouchables wanted local power, following Marks lead, we became obsessed with national and even the international dominance that Mark seemed destined to acquire.

Mark came home that summer from Yale stranger than ever. On any given Sunday, he could be seen in the den, practically in a trance, as he read the Wall Street Journal, Fortune Magazine or The New York Times. While the rest of the neighborhood engaged in mortal water balloon combat in his backyard, he watched documentaries on successful businessmen all day and night.

SUCCESS = I + C + R

I used to sit and watch him through the long glass sliding doors in the backyard as he inhaled the information in the newspaper and those boring business channels on television. What made him tick? He was strange, but intriguing none the less.

THE MOST POWERFUL TOOL KNOWN TO MAN IS THE SPOKEN WORD.

SOCIAL WORK

&

SIX DEGREES OF SEPARATION IS A BELIEF THAT EVERY PERSON IN THE WORLD IS ACCESSIBLE TO YOU THROUGH SIX PEOPLE. ONE OF THEM YOU ALREADY KNOW.

The social scene at the Erickson house slowly changed with Mark's acceptance into his new fraternal brotherhood. It was like Mark was a general in the Army, as carloads of people from all across the country would show up at the Erickson home to pay their respects on a daily basis. The traffic increased with each passing year and upon graduation, Mark was such a hot commodity, he was practically on fire.

He earned himself nationwide popularity by becoming the first person to become a Kappa Alpha Phi fraternity member on Yale's campus. This legitimized Mark, as well as putting the fraternity into an Ivy League category throughout the country. Mark's name and legacy would now live on forever. He sold himself in a package deal with Yale and his nationwide fraternity members to adoring admirers all across the nation. We could not believe what was happening right before our eyes. His twin brothers took it all in stride though.

It was like Mark was the godfather, and in an effort to capitalize off of his incredible popularity, the Erickson brothers started doing parties all across the country. I met so many celebrities and models at their parties, for a moment, I believed I was a celebrity as well. And just when I thought he could not possibly take his popularity any further, Mark in a move that shocked us all, left to serve additional time in Harvard University's Graduate School for Business Administration.

I was afraid the big year round party would end without him, but the twins picked up the slack as they pledged the same fraternity as their brother, solidifying the power of the entire family. I chose not to pledge as the hazing process reminded me too much of my run in with the Untouchables years prior. Although I reaped some of the social rewards bestowed upon the Erickson brothers by being their high school friend, to this day, not pledging is one of the worst, most regrettable choices I have ever made.

Two years flew by as the twins picked up the ball and ran with it. They continued to throw parties, even more extravagant than before. Their influence and power stretched from New York, to Los Angeles, to Miami. With a large group of loyal followers, major companies, anxious to introduce their commodities to the public, paid them to give away their products for free. They were becoming commodities dealers right before my very eyes.

Mark was not home for more than a week from graduate school when success tracked him down and made him an offer just too good to refuse. He got the call from the godfather of popular music himself. The man who had single-handedly turned Michael Jackson into the King of Pop, Mr. Quincy Jones.

Mr. Jones offered Mark the CEO position of Quest Records. Mark was no longer dealing commodities in parties. Now, he was a Sales Engineer, responsible for producing human commodities and selling them to the entire world. A few days later, Mark pulled me into the den and told me why he had been blessed with the opportunity of a lifetime.

"Bintell, do you know why I chose to go to Yale and Harvard and then to pledge a national fraternity?"

"Because they are good schools and you wanted to throw parties," I replied?

"No! Well, no to part of it, and yes to the other. Yes, they are good schools. Great schools, but more importantly, these schools are just a big boys club; and girls club too. They are clubs for the movers and shakers of tomorrow. In many ways, they are just like a gang?"

"So you did not study when you were there?"

"Oh my God I studied. They pledged us hard at Harvard. Only, they did not pledge us physically. They pledged us mentally."

"Really Mark?"

"Yes, being hazed was easy. After a while, taking physical pain was nothing." He stood up and stuck his chest out. Then he said, "Go ahead. Punch me in the chest as hard as you can!" I reluctantly leaned back, and threw my best punch at him. To my surprise, my fist bounced off of his chest like a ping-pong ball. He did not even blink. He just started talking again.

"The hard part was the mental abuse they put us through. The fraternity and Harvard were after the same thing. They wanted to see if we would quit under pain and pressure. To lead, you must be able to take pain. Pain is the thing that most people fear. If you can take pain, and come out the other end successfully, people will listen to you as they know you are capable of leading them through it---pain that is."

"So college and pledging was teaching you to take mental pain?"

"Exactly! The future leaders of the largest companies go to Harvard and Yale and schools like them. If I go to school with these people, they are not only my roommates, they are my friends? All these people that you see we know from our fraternity. They are not just my friends, they are now my brothers."

"Umm, I see…"

"And would you help me because you are my friend? Even more so, if you were my brother?"

"Of course Mark? I would do anything for you!"

"Well, they feel the same way Bintell. And Mr. Jones

knows that if the future CEOs of tomorrow are my friends, and even better, my brothers, it is in his best interest to be my friend too. Get it?"

I smiled and shook my head "Yes." Mark smiled and patted me on the shoulder. For some reason, he always wanted to tell me his little secrets. It was like I was his little pet project.

Years later, after he successfully engineered the careers of major pop stars and was living high up in the Hollywood Hills, Mark told me that running a large company, reminded him a lot of girls selling cookies for The Girl Scouts.

As Mark explained the similarity, I was reminded of my first sales job to raise money for our big end of the year play in elementary school. My favorite teacher Mr. Gullucio's proved to be more than just a teacher. He ended up being my first sales manager as well. After working and finding a few pockets of success as a Sales Engineer, I slowly realized just how right Mark actually was.

LOCKED AWAY IN A CELL, ALONE, SENTENCED TO SOLITARY CONFINEMENT, OVER TIME, CAN DRIVE THE MOST HARDENED CRIMINAL, ABSOLUTELY INSANE...

BIRTH OF AN ECONOMY

❧

TAKE THE AVERAGE SALARIES OF THE (5) PEOPLE CLOSEST TO YOU AND THAT'S HOW MUCH MONEY YOUR MACHINE IS PROBABLY GIVING YOU.

Although I failed miserably as a computer salesman in my adult life, the sales experiences I survived ironically mirrored those of my childhood. As a young boy in elementary school selling cookies, I was as much of a sales superstar as anyone I have ever worked with in the rat race. Well, maybe I was more like second runner up.

My sales career really began as a contest to raise money for our big end of the year school play, care of Mr. Gullucio. The play was only one month away, and the school's budget was tapped. We desperately needed money for costumes and props for various scenes, so a group of young salespeople in the making answered the call.

Just weeks before our big night, Mr. Gullucio made the announcement. "The school budget has been exhausted, so the principal is asking us to pitch in and help pay for the plays extra expenses by raising money selling cookies. Let's see who can sell all their cookies in time to make this play the success it should be." It felt like third and goal in the final 10 seconds of a football game's fourth quarter. The pressure was on.

Mr. Gullucio gave everyone their booklet of 25 raffle tickets worth $2 each. I asked for two booklets, as I knew exactly how I was going to save the day the minute he announced the contest.

> *Pressure is a challenge to achieve success, in a short amount of time*

Like many a sales director has done to inspire competition in their sales organization, Mr. Gullucio said, "Bintell is going to be the hero and sell two booklets. Let's see if anyone can keep up with him?" His plan worked like a charm. In the spirit of competition, two of the other kids with starring roles tried to outdo me. Michael Peterzack asked for 50 tickets, while Eileen Garavantee asked for 100.

I laughed under my breath at the nerve of them trying to keep up with me, much less outsell me. They would never sell that many tickets by the end of the week. Little did they know, I knew just who to hire to run my sales team the minute Mr. Gullucio made the job public. My 50 tickets would be sold without me breaking a sweat, as Mom and Dad would be the first sales team I would manage.

I came home and called an emergency meeting at the dinner table. As I explained the urgency of teamwork and the need to manage our time, Mom and Dad listened intently, shaking their heads up and down. I was as intense as any sales manager in the history of the rat race. Before the end of dinner, I had my first President's Club winning sales team trained and ready to go.

My mother immediately got on the phone, calling aunts and uncles all over the city. Dad said he would wait until he got to work before beginning his sales campaign. Mom on the other hand set up a tightly meshed distribution unit, spreading throughout all the boroughs of the greater New York area. Her partners were so enthusiastic to prove how much they cared for me, they kept her on the phone for an hour with feedback on how many tickets they would sell and by when. Ah yes, it would not be long before I was standing in the President's Club Circle, collecting my shiny trophy, bonus, and all expense paid trip. I started rehearsing my acceptance speech that night.

In two days, my mother and father sold all of my tickets to their friends, co-workers and family members. It was like taking candy from a baby it was so painless and easy. When I proudly showed up to school two days later with my tickets sold, holding a thick envelope full of cash and two empty booklets where ticket stubs were once attached, I was shocked to see that one of my co-stars had been far more successful than me. How could this be?

When Eileen Garavantee, the leading lady in our play announced that her mother, a regional director for a nationwide sales organization called Mary Kay had managed to sell 100 tickets in the space of two days, I could not believe my ears. Then, to add insult to injury, she said, "I can sell another 100 if you need me to." I ran to Mr. Gullucio's desk to watch him count the money in her envelope. There had to be some mistake. Selling that amount of tickets in that amount of time was impossible for one person.

But somehow she had done it. Every ticket had been signed and the envelope was stuffed with crisp $20 bills, totaling $200. How could this be? Eileen was in school with me all day and she only had her mother to help her. I had both my parents, so how did she sell more than me?

When I got home, I ran into the garage where my father could always be found bent over with his face inside someone's car engine. "Dad, Eileen sold more tickets than you and Mom. She said her mother works for Mary Kay. Doesn't that woman next door work for Mary Kay? Why didn't we ask her to help us?"

My father looked up from the car's engine and wiped the oil from his hands. "Mary Kay is a very big company. It is just your mother and I working for you. Eileen and her mother had resources my Boy. Human resources. She did not sell more tickets because your mother and I didn't work hard for you. She just had a better operation than we did. You have nothing to be ashamed of."

Being outsold by my co-star hurt my young ego so much, the lesson would linger in the back of my mind for years to come. You would have thought once I was a salesman, that old lesson learned would have saved me time floundering, but later on, working in the rat race, I got burned again and again in the same way. Finally, I realized relationships, strategic and profitable ones were the keys to turning commodities into money. Choosing the right one was the only issue, as they came in so many shapes and sizes.

The more I opened my eyes to the value of relationships, the more I realized that relationships that sold commodities all over the world were really what connected national and international economies. Having access to the various types of relationships made me feel like a kid in a candy store because now I knew, when successful people needed to turn a product into tons of money, they simply picked one.

Here is a list of all the most valuable, money-making relationships available to you with a description of how you can use them. Now, all you have to do is pick one.

"OUR BUSINESS IS ABOUT TECHNOLOGY, YES. BUT IT'S ALSO ABOUT OPERATIONS AND CUSTOMER RELATIONSHIPS."

- MICHAEL DELL

KID IN A CANDY STORE

&

"I REALLY WANT PEOPLE TO KNOW THAT I HAVE WORKED HARD, VERY HARD, TO GET TO WHERE I AM TODAY... THIS DID NOT JUST HAPPEN OVERNIGHT. I STARTED IN BUSINESS OVER 25 YEARS AGO AND HAVE FOUND A WAY TO BUILD ON WHAT I HAVE LEARNED THROUGH EVERY PARTNERSHIP AND OPPORTUNITY."
- MAGIC JOHNSON, GREATEST POWER FORWARD IN THE HISTORY OF BASKETBALL... SUCCESSFUL BUSINESSMAN

Putting your money machine in high gear, and selling tons of pain relief throughout the world, is all a matter of choosing the right relationships to help you. If you make the right relationship choices while building your money machine, your only job will be to sit back and catch all the money and success that will come flying out of it on a daily, weekly, monthly, quarterly or yearly basis. With the right relationships connected to your money machine, you will feel just like a kid in a candy store. Only this candy store will be full of money.

When I realized how valuable relationships were to the high speed money machines of the rich and powerful, my only question was, "Why didn't anyone tell me how many relationships there are to choose from before?"

This is one of the reasons I decided to write this book. So you will not have those same growing pains. For you, your biggest problem will be choosing which relationship to pick. To give you a head start in this process, I am here to tell you, the first relationship you will need as part of your money machine is, the media.

THE MEDIA

The media is the informative glue that holds our modern world together. For you, the media is just another piece of your money machine. The media is selling information as its primary and secondary commodity. Think of each media outlet as a separate salesperson that will sell your commodity for you better than you could ever sell it yourself.

> *Sales is a numbers game. The one percent rule is a success formula. It says one percent of the people who are in pain and can be cured by your product that see it in the media, will actually go out and buy it*

The media is doing the same thing everyone else in this $14 trillion money machine is doing, which is selling commodities. Once you have your new pain-relieving commodity in hand, the first part of your money machine you need to assemble is a sturdy piece of the media. Without the media your money machine will breakdown before you get it out of the driveway. Your commodity is invisible to those that will turn it into money if the media does not get involved. Remember, people cannot buy what they do not see.

If the media buys your commodity, and it actually relieves the pain you say it will, it is instantly hot. The job of the media is to tell people what commodities they should trust, and which ones they should avoid at all cost. The people who will go to the stores and buy your product, trust the media more than they will ever trust anything you could ever say about it. Once you earn the trust of the public with that first commodity, all other commodities you offer the public will be trusted on sight. As a result, you and your commodities will become trusted brands.

The good news is, the media needs your commodity just as much as your commodity needs the media. If media outlets do not have shiny new hot commodities to bring to its customers hungry for pain relief, they will find a media outlet that does, quickly.

The last thing any media outlet wants to be is, late or God forbid, missing in action to the hot commodity story. Their viewers depend on them to get the information first. The media works best when all media outlets are all working to sell your commodity at the same time. You want the media to surround the public with as much information of your commodity's pain relief for as long a period of time as possible.

The most effective/popular media outlets are:

1. Television
2. Magazine
3. Radio
4. Internet / Email
5. Newspaper
6. Direct Mailers
7. Billboards
8. Text to cell phone

Success = Media + Any Commodity + The World = **$$$**

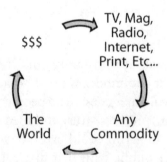

The reason people trust the media to help them make their choices to buy things is simple. The media is chock full of role models who are trained every minute of every day to be on their best behavior. People trust that if a commodity is not the real thing, these part-time role models, part-time commodity critics, will jump at the smallest opportunity to expose an untrustworthy commodity before anyone makes the mistake of buying it.

The news reports on commodities from celebrities, to entertainment, to the weather, to newly discovered healthy foods that can cure illnesses. Emails pop up in your inbox about commodities of all sorts. Bloggers write about human commodities on social networking sites like Facebook, Twitter, and MySpace, while websites act as 24 hour, seven day a week commercials for commodities of all sorts, with a built in check-out counter.

You as well as your commodity must maintain a healthy, long-term relationship with as many of these media outlets to ensure an even healthier relationship with other business partners responsible for your products hand-to-hand sale. If you do not nurture media relationships, your sales partners will struggle to sell your commodities or even worse, ignore it to sell a product owned by someone that does.

Information distribution by the media is an invaluable piece of your money machines success. The amount and type of information the media sends out about your commodity has a direct affect on how quickly your money machine spins, as well as the amount of money your machine will give you. If you and your commodity become what they call, a "media darling," it will be a trusted brand in the eyes of those who buy it. The first relationships that will come running to help you make all your dreams of success a reality will be the resellers.

RESELLER

With the media on your commodity's side, the first relationships that should jump inside your money machine are the resellers. Resellers know more than anyone, that if your commodity has been blessed by the media, the pain relief hungry consumer will buy it at a reasonable price point called the MSRP, which stands for Manufacturer Suggested Retail Price.

Resellers do exactly what their name suggests. They purchase your commodity with the intention of re-selling it for a profit. As a CEO, they are essentially a sales team you do not have to pay a salary and spend time managing. They buy the product at a discount, and sell it for the price you decide.

They are also great partners, as they are responsible for the storage, maintenance and depending on how hot it is, the cost to ship it to them. If the product relieves pain and you choose the right reseller, giving it to them at the right price, with the right information from the media, they can turn it into a hot commodity all over the world. When resellers are not sure in the value of the other parts of your money machine, they may choose to buy it through a distributor.

The distributor is like an insurance policy for your commodity to the reseller. The good news is, if you have the right distributor built into your money machine, they can convince the skeptical reseller of your product's hot commodity appeal with little to no time and energy spent by you.

<u>DISTRIBUTORS</u>

A distributor is basically a company that has relationships with the "retail" stores people will actually go to and purchase your commodity. Depending on the type of pain your commodity relieves, tens of thousands of retail stores may want to help you turn it into money. You on your own could not possibly keep track of all the money thousands of resellers will owe you. This is the pain relief the distributor will provide for you.

The distributor manages your supply chain. This is the cost of shipping, storage, payments from retailers and so on. This supply chain cost can eat into the profits from the sale of your commodity, so any company that can help you keep this cost low, is a relationship you MUST keep on your good side.

The distributor will charge you 40, 50, sometimes even 60 percent off the cost of your commodity as their fee, so keep this in mind when you are choosing a distributor, and assigning a price point for your commodity.

Distributors are simply protecting the retailers. If a CEO or president does not use the media to make sure his/her commodity is visible to the public, it will sit on the shelves and the retailer will be stuck with it. If the retailer buys products that have no chance of becoming a hot commodity, the retailer will lose so much money, they will soon go out of business. For this reason, successful retailers only make choices to stock their shelves with commodities that are insured by a distributor.

Distributors have no loyalty to any one commodity. They will provide their services to your competitors as this is a free market for all commodity providers. The only way you can get them to pay more attention to you is by building your money machine with a commodity that relieves more pain than anyone else's, and with more information to sell than the competition. Clever presidents and CEOs add a few dollars in the price of their commodity to pay for these situations. They refer to these costs to keep their commodity hot as R&D, and M&A, known as Research and Development and Marketing and Advertising respectively.

WHOLESALER

Wholesalers are like distributors less the insurance for the retailer. The wholesaler buys the commodity from you in large quantities. Because they are buying such large quantities from you, they will expect a very, very aggressive price for each commodity they buy. The reason you as the owner of your commodity will give them such a deep discount is, they have relationships with hungry retailers who will pass on the discount to their customers and get it sold. Unlike the distributor, once they buy it, they will never return it.

Wholesalers usually get involved with commodities called, "perishable goods" like food, flowers, fertilizer, paint and lumber for building houses.

Success = M&A + Product + (Wholesaler $ Retail Stores) = **$$$**

DEALERS

Dealers are very similar to resellers except, usually, they only sell one brand of commodity and usually, they only buy what they know they can sell or even better, place orders with you, as their customers place orders with them.

The sales strategy of selling one brand of commodity tells their buyers this dealer is just as interested in servicing the commodity should it need repair later on, as selling it for a profit now. Most dealers make the majority of their money from servicing the commodity in the long term, as opposed to selling it.

The most famous brand of dealership is the car dealer. A dealership will sell new commodities as well as old or refurbished ones. It may also stock and sell spare parts, and process warranty claims for the original owners that usually last one year from the original time of purchase.

The lines between dealers and resellers are becoming more and more difficult to decipher. Dealers hungry to reap the benefits of various competing brands (commodities), will sell and service more than one commodity in order to give the perception as being all things, to all people. At times, this strategy can backfire if there are not enough talented people with information on various commodities to deal with customer issues in a timely fashion.

Although dealers can see increased sales due to more commodity availability, they run into problems with managing and maintaining the back end servicing that goes along with each commodity's long-term commitment to their customers.

When choosing a dealer to assist you in selling your commodity, make sure they have a clear, well thought out process for handling such issues, as it could affect the level of trust and the reputation of your commodity in the eyes of those who you are trying to sell it to.

NETWORK GROUPS

Networking Groups are usually small intimate organizations that come together with the sole intention of passing leads between each other. These groups provide a healthy social outlet for their members, as successful people usually find themselves pressed for time. Small business owners usually perform more than one job description to get their money machines to run smoothly. Networking groups provide social as well as financial success for their members.

These groups usually allow only one member from any industry to join, to ensure there is no shortage of business for its members. They meet once a week in a central location and their meetings usually run an hour, two at most. During these meetings, each member has to stand and ask for a business opportunity, or offer a business opportunity to one or more of the group's members. There is a membership fee to join these groups. If the cost to join the group is not 10, tops 20 percent of the return on your investment, the Networking Group is probably not right for you and your commodity.

On the other hand, if you join one of these groups and do not have business to offer its members, you will probably be asked to leave quickly. When I got close to the superstar salespeople I have worked with over my career, I found out they were members of not just one, but quite a few Networking Groups.

THE CHANNEL PARTNER

Channel Partners are very similar to dealers. They are simply dealers that can move around. Like dealers, they buy a prescribed amount of your product just as a cost of doing business with you. They will come looking to become a part of your money machine based on customers requesting your product. Like dealers, their main goal is to help sell and market your product to become a hot commodity.

Dealers are usually found in a central location where people can come in and view the products they are selling, while channel partners are mobile and can come to the customer.

Channel partners like dealers are usually trained and certified by you to your satisfaction. This ensures that when the channel partner goes out and begins installing, selling and marketing your commodity, you as the owner can be sure the customer will be taken care of in a manner that will ensure repeat business. The goal is to make the customer feel as if they are buying the commodity/product right from you.

Channel partners and dealers are outside sales and marketing extensions of your company you do not have to pay a salary to. Channel partners are very popular in the world of information technology because computer systems usually need a person on staff to make sure they are functioning properly on

SUCCESS = I + C + R

a daily basis. From a sales perspective, they are like the copier salespeople I worked with as a Sales Engineer for Canon USA. Their customers trust them wholeheartedly.

AGENTS

Agents are simply salespeople who sell commodities for one or more companies, but are not employed by any company. They are independent, commission only salespeople. They are the purest form of a salesperson on Earth.

They live and die by the trust their customers have in them. If they betray that trust even once, they are practically out of business, as they do not get a paycheck from you. Because they do not require a paycheck, they require a healthier commission on the back end to get them to work for you.

If a salesperson's time is his/her most valuable commodity other than the commodity he/she is selling, an agent's time is priceless. He/she will only work to sell the commodities of those that pay the healthiest commissions, and relieve pain for their customers without fail.

REFERRAL PROGRAM

The referral program is simply your customers who are so happy with the commodity they have purchased from you, they inspire their friends and family to purchase one as well. This is the purest form of *The Formula* at work. This is where success begins to chase you. In business they call it, "word of mouth." Word of mouth is the most powerful brand of information to sell on earth.

To keep this successful sales momentum alive, some commodity owners employ the gold rule of sales and make sure there is something in it for their customers to keep talking about their commodity. They simply pay a small commission called a referral fee for every sale a former customer brings to them.

If the commodity is a service like a cab ride, shining shoes, washing cars, or tailoring of a garment, the commodity owner may choose to give a discount on future service. They may also choose to give a free service for a set amount of referrals.

LICENSING

Licensing is one of my favorite success producing relationships. Maybe it is because licensing has been used to sell me high-priced status symbols I really couldn't afford for years.

Licensing is completely dependent on the media to work properly. If there is not a healthy amount of information to sell the commodity and more importantly, its creator, licensing as a money-making relationship will never work.

Licensing is used frequently in the clothing industry. In the clothing or textile industry, licensing is basically reselling a brand, specifically, the label or the actual tag inside the garment. When clothing designers make what they call "aspirational clothing," it allows the working class to dress and model themselves after the wealthy. For this to work, they must allow the media to show their elegant clothes to the world.

These clever creators stage well-publicized fashion shows as the most beautiful fashion models strut about in their tailored ever so elegant clothing. They invite the most popular celebrities in music, film, and every section of high society to attend. Working class people desperate to get their hands on a small piece of the American Dream, drool over these clothes as they feel getting their hands on the clothing is getting a piece of the good life.

After the media has turned their fashion shows into a worldwide circus, these clever designers then sign licensing deals with a multitude of unknown designers allowing them to put their labels on their clothes. The labels are simply their names, as people are buying a piece of the actual designer and the lifestyle they represent. The top clothing designers can then sell each licensing deal for millions. Some of them sell 20 licensing deals per season, turning themselves into multi-millionaires in a very short period of time.

When the consumer walks into a store and sees a piece of clothing with the tag of the designer they have seen in a well publicized fashion show, they buy it instantly. This relationship between designer and licenser worked on me like a formula for success for years. I would say, "Hey, look at this sweater. I am going to get it. It's made by XYZ designer. It's a steal at this price!"

PRODUCT PLACEMENT

Product placement is simply the sales model of putting a commodity in a movie or television show so millions of people can see it and understand how it cures pain. The information to sell comes from simply seeing it with its logo on television.

Television shows full of trusted celebrities and successful people on their best behavior can evoke enough trust in any commodity to send its sales through the roof. Technology companies like Cisco and Apple have and continue to use this formula successfully to almost eliminate the competition. The lines between product placement and movie merchandising can blur so much, it is hard to tell them apart.

Success = Appear on TV + Commodity / Stars + Viewing Audience = **$$$**

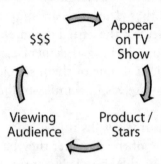

<u>MERCHANDISING</u>

With all this talk about the media and how instrumental it is as a business relationship, it is only fitting that we now examine the business relationship called merchandising. Merchandising is the use of popular movies to sell commodities that are somehow related to the movie.

Because movies are full of human models that teach us how to behave, dress, and achieve success in the most heroic and emotional of fashions, it's not surprising that young and old, eager to get their hands on a small piece of success they see in these movies, purchase anything even slightly associated with them.

This phenomenon of selling pieces of a movie is known as merchandising, with its distant cousin being product placement. There are lots of stories of people from humble beginnings using merchandising and product placement to create wild success for themselves. One great story is that of Salvatore Ferragamo.

The wedge shoe was a natural evolution of the famous high-heeled shoe called the pump. A simple and genius invention, the wedge design was to simply put cork underneath the entire shoe, adding support for all those women who could not walk in the high heel pump. With the addition of the soft cork, now, women who could not walk and support themselves in the fragile pump shoe, found added support as well as the height of the pump they so desperately desired.

If anyone was destined to discover the wedge heeled shoe, it was Mr. Ferragamo. Always passionate about making shoes less painful for women who wore them, Mr. Ferragamo studied anatomy and physiology even after his business was thriving. How he managed to move to America from Florence Italy and rise to the highest position of celebrity shoe design was largely due to his relationship with Hollywood.

Salvatore opened a shop for repair and made-to-measure shoes in Hollywood fueled by relationships he made working for the American Film Company. Soon his shoes were the talk of the town with top celebrities of the day like Maharani of Cooch Behar to Eva Peron to Marilyn Monroe, leading to a long period of designing footwear for the cinema. Salvatore's thriving reputation as 'Shoemaker to the Stars' accelerated his small company right into the fast lane of high-end shoe design using the magical red shoes in the world famous movie The Wizard of Oz, (which Mr. Ferragamo designed) as information to sell his commodity to millions of people throughout the world.

The small Ferragamo shoe company grew in leaps and bounds. Mr. Ferragamo confident in his success, moved back to his birthplace and true to behavior of success and *The Formula*, relationships followed him home. Celebrities would fly across oceans as they desperately needed Mr. Farragamo's pain free shoes to be successful in their upcoming films. With his business booming, Mr. Farragamo outdid himself and invented the cage-heeled shoe, catapulting his already successful business into a multi-billion dollar worldwide lifestyle brand.

Success = Movies + Shoes & Movie Stars + Celebrity Crazed Public = **$$$**

$$$ → Info from Movies

Celebrity Crazed Public ↑   ↓ Shoes & Movie Stars

After a few spins of ***The Formula***, Mr. Ferragamo had successfully re-invented his humble shoe company into a full scale luxury lifestyle brand, now providing commodities from furniture, to wine, to shoes, to men's and women's clothing. Mr. Ferragamo is an example of a timeless success story.

Merchandising relationships have produced millions and billions in movies like Star Wars, Shrek, Dora The Explorer, Harry Potter, Iron Man and Spiderman.

BANKS

Banks are just another part of the money machine. Banks supply a commodity called money, to help your money machine make of all things, more money. They are just another relationship inside your formula.

As information, other commodities and relationships are put to work to sell commodities for successful people, banks see money as a commodity to be put to work as well.

The banks will ask you for a thing called a "business plan", which is basically an outline of how your money machine is put together.

A good business plan will include the assembly instructions of a well-oiled money machine designed by you. Banks want to know that your money machine's design has eliminated as much risk as possible so they know, they will get their money back and then some which they call interest. The big question on their minds is, when.

Banks are interested in one thing, more money. They are the purest form of a money machine, as the commodity they are selling happens to be money. If they believe your money machine is designed properly and understand the value of the commodity inside it, they will happily give you enough money to acquire all the other parts of your money machine needed to create wild success.

All banks ask in return is interest on the money they lend you in an agreed upon amount of time. The good news is, if you design a well-oiled money machine, in their eyes, money is no object as they have an almost unlimited supply.

ENDORSEMENT DEALS

The endorsement deal is probably one of the most publicized business relationships of the modern day. It is also the purest form of selling trust to create success and lots of money. Athletes like Michael Jordan, and LaBron James have put their personal money machines into overdrive by choosing the right endorsement relationships. Although the contracts for these talented athletes pay them millions of dollars, the most talented athletes have been reported to make $100 million each year in endorsements alone.

The endorsement deal is all about a talented human commodity selling other commodities. Famous successful people can sell non-living commodities and they can also sell human commodities as is done most of the times in politics.

When people are not sure they trust a new perfume, a car, or even an unknown brand of bug spray, clever CEOs put money to work and buy relationships with trusted athletes, actors and actresses to endorse their commodity and sell a lot of it.

With the help of the media and these trusted personalities, commodity sales usually fly off the charts. The most famous and powerful endorser to date is Oprah Winfrey. Economists have talked about the Oprah effect, as she is so trusted by her audience, she has been known to turn unknown commodity owners into multi millionaires in a matter of days.

NETWORK MARKETING

Network marketing companies do exactly what their name suggests. They use a network of people to market various products quickly. They work just like any sales organization I have ever worked for. The only difference is, the entire organization is full of commission only salespeople.

There is usually one person at the top who stands to be the most successful. In a company, this person is usually the VP of Sales. As he/she hires people underneath them who are expected to use their personal and professional relationships to sell, sell, sell, their success grows and grows. The more relationships they add to their money machines, the more money their machine spits out for them.

This pyramid model for money machine design makes sense of the picture of an eye at the top of the pyramid on the dollar bill that confused me so much as a young boy.

CORPORATE PARTNERSHIPS

To explain the corporate partnership, I'll tell a quick story about one of my many summer experiences in the playground for the wealthy, famous and powerful, the Hamptons.

One summer I managed to end up at a party in the Hamptons for the godfather of hip-hop music himself, Mr. Russell Simmons. How I ended up there without my social wing man Jason, I could not tell you.

It was a cool summer's night and although many a "nerd" from the corporate world would have been jumping for joy sitting at Mr. Simmons' table with his close friends, I took it all in stride.

Sitting in the mid summers air of the Hamptons, Mr. Simmons and one of his long time business partners unknowingly gave me a tip on how they were using **The Formula** to build a high speed money machine together.

To my left sat an older woman and her husband. To my right sat my girlfriend and to her right sat an actor from one of my favorite success movies, the Thomas Crown Affair.

The older man with his wife called Russell over to whisper in his ear about something one of the guests was wearing. While they were talking, trying to make small talk, his wife asked me, "Son, what is it that you do?"

"I am an engineer for a technology company."

"Okay. That's interesting. Do you like it?"

"It's a living I guess. Your husband is friends with Russell Simmons. He must be very successful. What does he do?"

Without blinking an eye she said, "He owns North Face. The goose down jackets people wear." I said "Okay, I love those jackets," trying to hide how stunned I was to be so casually sitting next to such wealthy people. The humble couple was not as famous as Russell Simmons, but they were just as successful if not more.

That summer ended after quite a few parties and as usual, the winter came blowing into the New York City streets, forcing everyone to bundle up. Then one cold Monday in January while walking down the street, I realized the value of the relationship between Russell Simmons and the owner of North Face.

As I walked two blocks past 34th Street to take another train uptown, I saw at least fifteen young kids who looked like they loved hip-hop music wearing Phat Farm goose down jackets. The strange thing about these jackets was, they looked exactly like the North Face jackets worn by the older, more mature crowd I had seen skiing in Connecticut. That was when it hit me. Phat Farm and North Face had come together and used information, or should I say, branding to design a healthy amount of success for themselves.

Russell Simmons cleverly used North Face to manufacture the commodity, and North Face cleverly used the Phat Farm logo to sell them. In the world of information technology, we did the same thing. The products that we produced and sold in this way were called assemblies.

Success = Logo + Clothing + Music Lovers = **$$$**

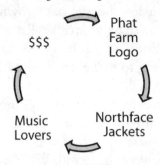

If you keep your eyes peeled, you'll see that these corporate partnerships are very, very common.

<u>POLITICS</u>

Politics has to be the highest point in all of wealth, fame and power by way of relationships. Politics is arguably the DNA of success. As far as the free markets are concerned, politicians sell themselves to the public at-large as a product that will ease their social and financial aches and pains.

If the information they distribute through the media makes them appears trustworthy, they are purchased with the currency of a vote. If they successfully sell themselves into political power, they are given the honor and privilege of becoming supreme rulers of all commodities in their territory.

SUCCESS = I + C + R

Success = Information + Politician + Voters = **Majority Votes**

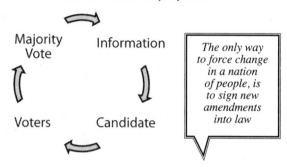

Once a politician is voted into power, they are responsible for passing laws that will ensure a fair and even distribution of commodities for those that voted for them. These laws are designed to ensure a prosperous and peaceful existence for the people of the land. If politicians do not pass these laws, and if the information from competing politicians convinces voters they are not trustworthy, they will be voted out of office in one term.

To ensure long-term success, politicians must listen closely to the feedback they get from media sources and polls that measure their popularity with voters. Politicians like products are owned by the people who buy them. Although the rules of campaigning are constantly changing to ensure the aches and pains of the people are heard, politicians are in many cases owned not just by the people, but also by large multi-billion dollar corporations of a country.

Large corporations supply politicians with unlimited supplies of money to buy tons of information to sell themselves to the public, putting them back into office. Large corporations supply politicians with this unlimited money supply for one reason. Once their politicians are in power, they are expected to pass laws that will make it ever so easy for the companies to make 10 times the amount of money they paid to get their politician in office.

Success = Laws + Various Commodities + (Corporation & Politician) = **$$$**

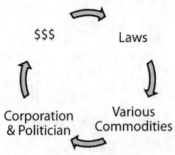

$$$ Laws

Corporation & Politician

Various Commodities

MERGERS & ACQUISITIONS

If there is any one relationship in all of business and money making that people fear and respect, yet know very little to nothing about, it is the merger and acquisition. Not to be confused with information that sells, M&A, also known as marketing and advertising. Mergers and acquisitions are the pinnacle of valuable relationships in business.

A merger and acquisition is basically when two companies come together as one. For owners of commodities desperate to either get a broken-down money machine to run as if it was new again, or to add extra horsepower to their already well-tuned money machine, mergers and acquisitions can be and have been used as a clever formula for success. There are pros and cons with any relationship. Here is some food for thought.

If a merger and acquisition is well designed, it could have a positive effect on the value of the information, the commodities and the strategic relationships of the owners of both companies. The right merger and acquisition can combine the secret information about selling, creating or identifying new tried and true commodities a company has for the purpose of sale and profit.

Additionally, mergers and acquisitions allow one company, usually the company doing the acquiring, to put their logo on the company's products they are acquiring. This is good for both parties because now, the company with the money machine on the verge of breaking down, has the instant trust of the stronger company it has merged with. The company that has done the acquiring gains relationships with more customers and that is always good for business.

Another benefit is Economy of Scale which means that both companies working as one can reduce the cost to create the commodity by eliminating duplicate pieces of their money machines. This is good for the company, but bad for the people working in the company as this usually means layoffs.

Economy of Scope is the amount of information (M&A) and relationships (Partners, Retailers, Agents, etc.) needed to sell and turn products into hot commodities. With two companies working as one these amounts are usually less and thus, money is saved.

Because of the increase in the size of the new company, larger orders of those commodities needed to create a final one goes down. The reason for this is simple. When you buy more of a commodity, you usually get a better discount because you are spending more money as you are buying more product. The rule is, low per unit, high per unit price and vice versa, high per unit, low per unit price. The other side of this rule says, high per unit output, low per unit price.

Tax benefits are also available. The company that is doing well can write off the losses of the company that is not doing well on their taxes. This success formula is called reducing tax liability. This means more money for the owners of the money machine come tax time.

Yet, with all of the obvious benefits that can come from the powerhouse relationship through mergers and acquisitions, there is a very, very serious potential for failure one should always take into consideration before building this type of relationship. The worst of them is conflict between the two cultures of each company.

As we now know, people will resist change tooth and nail. If there are different cultures in each company, they could clash and destroy both companies before they have a chance to succeed. The best example of a failed merger and acquisition is the multi-billion dollar failure of AOL/Time Warner.

COMMUNITIES

Although most people don't realize it, the community you live in is a very important and valuable social and economic relationship. The majority of information that we get comes from our immediate environment. Our communities are usually our best teachers. Our neighbors, schools and churches are the institutions that shape who we are and our future success. For me, the information I received on the South Shore was very different than the information I received on the North Shore.

The relationships we stumble upon in our communities shape our perception of success. Most people assume the aspirations for success from those that live with and around them. In a perfect world, those we live and grow with in our communities will share their success formulas and secrets with us. Our communities are the first fraternities we ever join.

Some of the longest lasting relationships that will supply us with the most valuable information we will ever encounter will be a direct result of the communities and neighborhoods we grow up in. My mother and I argue the point at least once a month that, had we not moved from the South Shore to the North Shore, would we have aspired to dream the dreams we have?

Would my sister have opened her own health care facility and would I have started my own publishing company had it not been for the examples I saw before me on the North Shore of Long Island New York? This is why they say, when you are buying real estate, it's all location, location, location. Taking

210

that a step further, people also say the comparison that comes from traveling from one place to another, is said to be the "best education."

<u>MARRIAGE</u>

For better or for worse. Till death do us part. It is the most important merger and acquisition of your life. It is the longest standing relationship known to man. Although many would argue this union is purely a relationship of the heart, others will say it is the most important business relationship choice you will ever make in your life.

Arguably the most misunderstood, most valuable commodity on Earth, marriage is a product designed to ease the emotional pain brought on by loneliness. Our need to express our love and be loved is satisfied by a union of the heart called marriage.

Unlike other business relationships that are usually 1, 2, 3, 4, or even 5 year commitments, marriage is a lifetime commitment. Many argue that when it comes to marriage, money should not be part of the negotiation. Others, those who are most times in control of the money machine that runs our lives, see things quite differently. One of the most famous marriages in the history of humanity is that of Caesar, the supreme ruler of Rome, and Cleopatra, the last Emperor of Ancient Egypt.

"Veni, vidi, vici." Short for, "I came, I saw, I conquered are the infamous words of the famed Julius Caesar. A man who's rise to power included a lust for violence and conquest by way of one of the most powerful military forces of its time, and changing Roman history forever. Add this to all the legendary timeless beauty and power of the infamous Cleopatra, famed female Pharaoh of the wealthy Ancient Egypt, and you have designed a formula for success.

Julius Caesar's rise to power included a bloody string of conquest that left his people hungry for the power and thrill of violence. He gave the people violence not only through the military, but also in the famed arena. He also achieved dictatorship status as the Emperor of Rome by installing his own associates in as many positions of government. So many powerful associates he had, he was in time able to re-write laws allowing him to remain in office. His relationship with famed beautiful Cleopatra was a function of his need for money to fund a war.

Cleopatra, a devoted public servant of her beloved Ancient Egypt, knew that a union between the most powerful military in the world, and the wealthiest country in the land through marriage would solidify the position of Egypt, as well as her offspring. So when Caesar came to Egypt in search of money to fund one of his many military campaigns, a relationship based on more than just finances resulted. Caesar and Cleopatra produced three children who if everything went according to plans, would inherit two empires and boundless success.

$$SUCCESS = I + C + R$$

Success = Laws Inheritance + (Egypt & Rome) + (Caesar & Cleopatra) = $$$

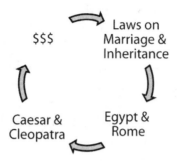

Unfortunately, Caesar's rise to power scared the Roman government and in time, he was assassinated. As a result, Cleopatra's plans for her children supreme power were dashed by the successor to Caesar, Octavian, causing her to commit suicide.

FRANCHISING

The word franchise means privileged, or freedom in the old French language. Buying into a franchise is like buying into a fraternity of an exclusive club. The most successful business in the world is a franchise. McDonalds is a picture perfect example of the power of franchising as the company doesn't just sell fast food, it also sells real estate to new franchise minded business people willing to buy into a successful business model.

Franchising is a method of doing business where a franchisor sells tested and proven methods of successfully doing business to a franchisee in exchange for a recurring payment, and usually a percentage piece of gross sales or gross profits as well as an annual fee.

The benefits of franchising are numerous from every aspect of *The Formula*. As the person buying into the franchise, you receive free national or international advertising information. You also get training so that you are aware of the latest and greatest in successful sales models for the commodity.

213

Buying into a franchise lets you off the hook as far as creating a commodity because that has already been taken care of for you. You do not need to create a business plan as it has already been written for you. It is like flying a plane on auto-pilot. For the most part, you are just along for the ride.

Because the franchisor has already spent millions, sometimes billions of dollars in marketing and advertising, there is no need to worry your head with branding your business. The site of the successful franchise logo will cause the customers that already trust it to come running.

Because buying into a franchise is essentially buying a share of stock in an already successful company, there are strict rules that you are required to follow. If you are looking to be your own boss and make your own choices to determine the future of your success, franchising may not be for you. Franchising can make you feel as though you are an employee at times as failure to abide by the rules of the franchisor can result in non-renewal or cancellation of franchise rights.

Now, let's have some fun running your company. Let's turn you into the president you should be. Just like my friend from the candy store years ago pointed out, if you want to make the big bucks, you have got to be your own boss. This is exactly how you are going to do it.

BUSINESS IS ALL RELATIONSHIPS

ACT NINE

Success = Information+ Commodities + Relationships = \$\$\$

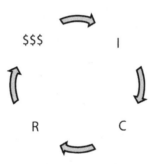

MASTER
MIND

HEAD HONCHO

಄

I f there is any one job in all of the rat race that strikes admiration, as well as fear in the hearts of working class men and women, it is that of the president and CEO. The man. The top dog. The head honcho. The person responsible for making all the tough choices. Salespeople call him/her the DM. He / she is also known as, The Decision Maker.

It had to be my first week as a salesman with no copier salespeople to help me when my new overly aggressive manager said, "Bintell, when you make your calls, always ask to speak to the president of the company. If you can get the president or the CEO on your side, you can sell anyone else in the company just about anything."

Well, it sounded easy enough to do. Just find out who the President is and ask to speak to him/her when you make that call. Okay, but if I was lucky enough to get them on the phone, what in God's name would I say?

If you asked me to call my mother and sell her something, I could do that. I knew my mother's aches and pains. I knew my mother needed anything that would help her with the washing of clothes, cooking, and getting my sister and me to school and to bed on time. But I had never met a CEO or president in my life other than Mark in high school and he had not prepped me on how to sell stuff to people like himself. For me, making calls to presidents and CEOs was like taking stabs in the dark and hoping for success.

The few times I was able to get through to a president or CEO, after they politely listened to me beg for a meeting while I tripped over my words for a minute or so, they would say, "Son, why don't you call my CIO (Chief Information Officer). Tell him I told you to call. If he finds value in your product, he will set up a meeting for us to talk at a later date." Those calls never resulted in a sale. It took me years to realize why.

One day, trying to keep myself from sleeping through yet another sales training class on a new job, somebody finally gave me the Holy Grail. They told me what makes a president and CEO tick.

The sales trainer for this job had taken us through a series of question and answer sales models designed to get the customer to put all their daily aches and pains out in front of them, and then, instead of you asking them to buy your commodity, they would be begging you to sell it to them. After one week and four days of practice, on the last and final day, he gave us the big CEO secret.

"Okay class, these two weeks of sales strategy have led you to the top of the mountain. You have been trained on how to talk to everyone in the company except the most important person, the president. I am here to tell you, all presidents and CEOs have only three aches and pains on their minds each and every day. If you can prove to them that you can help them cure these three pains, they will be your new best friend. They will give you a slice of their precious time called, a meeting." The three pains are:

1. **THE COST TO BRING THEIR COMMODITY TO MARKET.**
2. **THE COMPETITION.**
3. **SELLING THEIR COMMODITY TO MORE AND MORE PEOPLE.**

Years later with *The Formula* in my possession, I realized the three concerns of every president, CEO and top officer of any company on Earth, were simply the three parts of *The Formula*. So, how do they use the three parts of *The Formula* to make their companies successful?

(v)Information

1. COST TO BRING COMMODITY TO MARKET

Every person on Earth is a chief executive officer their lives and a member of the board in their family. You are a product you are bringing to market and so are your children. There is a cost associated with bringing yourself, and the members of your family to market for the purpose of sale. For most parents, one of the largest cost associated with bringing their children to market is their education.

Your job as the president of your life, as well as a parent, is to bring these human products to market with the least amount of money spent, while making sure you turn yourself and your children into the most valuable brand of person possible.

The best presidents and CEOs are always looking to keep the cost to create and sell their commodity of choice to a minimum, without destroying its value. The lower the cost to bring a product from creation to sale, the more money that will be left over for the owner to enjoy.

Savvy presidents and CEOs hire the most talented of people to work with and for them. People that can process information to successfully create or sell a product, in the shortest amount of time are valuable people to know. The golden rule is, the quicker a company can get these two things done, the more money they will have made for themselves, as time is money.

They also buy the commodities needed to create the final commodity from those who offer them the lowest price. If it makes sense, they will even pay another company to make their commodity in large amounts at the lowest possible price. This business model is called outsourcing.

Your job as a president or a CEO is to do this, while convincing the world that the product you are bringing to market is second to none in quality and thus, will relieve their pain without fail. If so, the people of the world will happily make you a very, very successful president and CEO.

(v)Commodity

2. ELIMINATE THE COMPETITION

There is never a product that doesn't have competition. Once people get wind of your product becoming a hot commodity, it will become a model for success and people will imitate it. In the spirit of moving forward, they will say, "Instead of doing it like that, what if we change it and made it just a little better?"

Good CEOs are always on the lookout for competing commodities that will steal their customers or worse, put them out of business. The government, those that are in charge of making sure this game of wealth, fame and power called capitalism love competition. They believe it gives people the best possible chance of purchasing a commodity at a fair price. Luckily, *The Formula* comes in handy in a number of ways to keep the competition at bay.

The best CEOs are always listening closely to the feedback

their customers provide them. Feedback added to the ideas they come up with on their own allows them to stay one, hopefully two steps ahead of the competition. When companies fail to listen to this feedback, their days at the top of the commodity pile are numbered.

The richest families in American history like the Rockefeller's or the DuPont's, or the Millin's and Carnegies are no longer the richest in the world due in most part to their inability to listen to feedback and re-invent themselves over time. As a result, companies like Microsoft, Ebay, Google, Oracle, and a whole host of newcomers have taken their place at the top of the top 9% of society.

The CEOs of Tower Records failed to listen to the feedback of their customers, choosing not to change their business model, and online retailers like iTunes put them out of business. In the world of IT, the same changes were taking place.

The CEOs of Nortel Networks, in their heyday, one of the largest information technology hardware providers had commodities so hot, the company was worth $400 billion and its stock was valued at $124.50 a share. They failed to listen to the feedback of their customers and in time, their company's value fell to $3 billion with a stock price of $1.24.

Cisco was listening intently to the feedback of their customers while Nortel was off being so successful, they ignored the people who had made them that way. Nortel Networks filed for bankruptcy while Cisco has taken over the entire IT world, and now slowly moving into the world of cell phones.

But feedback alone will not keep the competition from taking over your business. To be the best CEO possible, you must use the individual pieces of *The Formula* to keep the competition confused and on its toes. Here are some formulas for successful CEO-ship in a competitive marketplace.

Flood the media with information regarding the pain relief of your commodity.

Using the media to bombard the public about your commodity makes the competition appear invisible and makes your commodity appear trustworthy. The more information you use, the more of a preferred brand you and your commodity will become. As proof, the estimated budget for the US Marketing & Advertising in 2008 came in at $412 billion.

Surround your commodity with other trusted commodities.

The endorsement deal is a very effective way to set you and your commodity apart from the competition. When successful people, whether athlete, musician or movie star tell the world they depend on your product to relieve their aches and pains, all those that love and adore them, instantly love and adore your soon to be hot commodity. The same rules apply when companies decide to partner with each other successful companies around the sale of a particular commodity. This strategy is called, a strategic partnership.

When companies announce partnerships or even better, a merger and/or acquisitions, it increases their value almost instantly. People know that each company, with their loyal customers will now purchase the commodities of not one company, but both. Two companies working together make up for what each of them lack. If one is light in the information department, the other will pick up the slack.

Just the rumor of two titans of an industry forming an alliance can make traders, investors and speculators of their stock millions of dollars instantly.

Ramp up sales force.

Ramping up a sales force is not just a matter of hiring salespeople. With a wide array of strategic relationships available to the owner of a commodity, clever commodity owners take advantage of as many of them as possible to drown out the competition.

If you have more feet on the street selling your commodity, the probability of outselling the competition is very, very high.

(v)Relationships

3. SELL THE COMMODITY TO MORE AND MORE PEOPLE

Ultimately, CEOs and presidents are judged by sales. In these days of publicly traded companies whose stock prices go up and down each day, their success is measured solely by the amount of commodities they sell.

Because there is competition, you may have relationships with 20, 30 or even 40 percent of all the customers that buy commodities like yours. Most times, it is a struggle just to hold onto these customers called your market share. If you can manage to do this, your next thought as a CEO should be, "If we have four out of every 10 people that buy commodities like ours, how can we get the other 6?" The methods used to eliminate the competition will help you hold onto, and increase the market share of your commodity.

These days, with companies selling stocks to raise money for their next commodity offerings, CEOs are judged on keeping cost low. Some are judged by their ability to drown out the competition, while the best are worshiped for increasing market share. Whether they are able to achieve one, or all three

> "We can believe that we know where the world should go. But unless we're in touch with our customer, our model of the world can diverge from reality. There's no substitute for innovation, of course, but innovation is no substitute for being in touch, either."
> Steve Ballmer - CEO Microsoft

of the CEO goals, they are always concerned with achieving their success in the shortest amount of time. In the ever changing rat race of the American Dream, time, not money, is the final business frontier.

THE MOST VALUABLE COMMODITY TO A SALESPERSON IS HIS/HER TIME.

TIME MACHINE

&

WHEN SUCCESSFUL PEOPLE WEAR WATCHES WORTH TENS OF THOUSANDS OF DOLLARS, THEY ARE TRYING TO SAY TO THE WORLD, "MY TIME IS SO VERY VALUABLE, I NEED THIS EXPENSIVE TIMEPIECE TO HELP ME KEEP TRACK OF IT."

"A MAN WHO DARES TO WASTE ONE HOUR OF LIFE HAS NOT DISCOVERED THE VALUE OF LIFE."
                                              - CHARLES ROBERT DARWIN

Y**ou remember it. You remember how it felt. I know I will never forget it. The shock to my system when I realized 80, maybe even 90 percent of my time between Monday and Friday would be sacrificed in the name of a paycheck. I remember it like it was yesterday. How I swallowed it silently, my heart breaking, trying to hide my fear with a smile, crying inside with no tears, right before the person who had just given me exactly what I had come for, a job.

How my heart sank deep into my chest, practically into my stomach when I realized I had to stand still and allow The Man to put the tag on my toe for money. How I felt it was a no win situation when I realized how slow my money machine would go making minimum wage every hour. Well, if Captain Kirk thought space was the final frontier, on Earth, time my friends, this is a frontier if I ever saw one.

While doing my time at Northeastern University, there were a lot of time consuming formulas. To make matters worse, Northeastern was a trimester school.

This meant, information that other students at other

schools took five months to digest, we at Northeastern had to digest in three. Because of the rate of speed information was being hurled at you, Northeastern University's engineering program maintained an 80% dropout rate. Only God knows how I managed to survive this tidal wave of information and actual graduate.

Socializing and studying were out of the question for me. The engineering formulas were very long and complex leaving little time for much of anything else. So, to fit in the socializing I desperately needed, I decided to memorize the steps of the three-paged formulas and figure out what they meant later.

The formulas were models that always behaved a certain way. Once I could predict the way the formula behaved, getting the right answer was just like playing hopscotch, or learning a complicated dance.

Through the five years of formula after formula after formula, I noticed that in every one of them, there was always this little t. Regardless of the formula's shape, this t thing always managed to be a part of the mix. I could not seem to get rid of it. No matter what class I went to, this little t thing was following me.

It just would not go away. It was like a blinking red light trying to get my attention, or a fly buzzing in my ear. After a while, I gave in to the fact that it was not going to go away, so I found ways to dance over it and complete my work in time to get my degree. But in the back of my mind I knew, sooner or later, that t and I were going to come to blows.

I feared for the worst, as the t seemed to have relationships with every mathematical equation on Earth. Years later in the big interview for the Sales Engineering job with Canon USA, that little t rudely reached out and grabbed me by the collar once again.

I felt I was just as capable of doing a good job as anyone else, although I had no idea what I needed to do or say to be successful as a salesman. Rich Chereskin said, "You have got a strong background, but I am not sure you will be able to pick up the technology quick enough to gain the trust of the copier salespeople and survive here." I sat there looking into his eyes like a deer caught in headlights and after a few minutes of uncomfortable silence, for some odd reason, Rich smiled at me.

Next, he turned his laptop around and showed me an Excel spreadsheet linked to a database with the other three people he hired. It had their sales achievements laid out with color charts and graphs in what he called "real-time".

"Here are some salespeople I hired that have the same engineering background as you. Only one of them looks like he is not going to make it." Rich knew how much money they would be receiving in commissions and by when.

"Robert is on pace to make $200k, while Peter is on pace to make about $175k for the year," he explained as he pointed to the graphs on the laptop. "If I hire you today, six months from now, what will you be on pace to make by year's end? We have a free trip to Monte Carlo as a Presidents Club Level II prize for all the top salespeople. Do you think you will win?"

"Well Sir, that is a concern, but to that all I can say is, I did manage to graduate on time." An offer letter arrived at my house one week later.

I was not successful right off the bat. It took me a little figuring out, but after a while, I got the hang of it. New Years Eve of the year 2000 at 10:30PM, I signed the last $100,000 in time to win the trip to Monte Carlo. I would like to say I did it all on my own, but the truth is, my victory came with some help from the company superstar, Victor Williams. If I ever saw someone with a high speed money machine, Victor was it. He was a copier-sales Harry Houdini.

The whole company idolized him. Right from the first month I was on the job, he was pulling down commission checks of $100k and better every month. I would watch the board where all the salespeople put up their numbers every month and right before months end, Mr. Williams would casually put $500k,

$600k, and $800k up on the board like it was nothing. For some reason, he took a liking to me. He would sell my computers to his customers and make my quota without me having to lift a finger.

He was always moving fast with a smile on his face. People in the office used to tease him whenever they caught him by the water cooler. He would smile as they taunted him and say, "Every time I talked to Victor he is like, I got to shoot uptown and then shoot right back downtown."

Well this day Victor was in the office filling out some paperwork at his desk. Looking at him, you would never have known he was the top salesman in the company he was so easy going and approachable. This day I found the courage to ask him the question everyone had been dying to ask. I sat next to him, pulled my chair up close enough that he could not ignore me and said. "Victor?"

"What's up Bintell?"

"I need to know something." He seemed stunned but still smiled through the awkward moment.

"Yeah? What's eating you?'

"I need you to tell me right now, if you had to point to any one thing as the key to your success over the years, what would it be?" He stopped smiling and for the first time ever, Victor looked just like the CEOs I had seen interviewed on the Bloomberg Channel. He was not smiling anymore. He was deadly serious.

"Bintell, if you really want to know, I'll tell you. I am going to tell you this knowing you probably won't take it to heart, but since you have cornered me, I am going to tell you the big secret." He cleared his throat once or twice, looked around to see if anyone was listening, and then he bent down and spoke.

"Time."

"What Victor?"

"You heard me. Time. My time."

"What about it?"

"The way I choose to spend it. That's what makes me more successful than the next guy."

"How do you spend it Victor?"

"Well, it's more like who I choose to spend it on. If I had to point to any one thing, that would be it."

"Victor, I am serious. Tell me the truth."

"I am. You asked me and I gave you a serious answer. Now you don't want to hear it?"

"No! It just seems like you are pulling my leg. Is this a joke you are going to tell the branch about when I am not looking?"

"Listen, the product I am selling is not the point. It's the choices I make as to how I spend my time. I do not do anything, with anyone ever, unless I am convinced it's going to help me sell my product. My time is precious. If you waste it, you are wasting money. The people I spend my time on are not just friends, they are partners, customers, get it?"

"I think so."

"Well, you have 30 days each month to hit your number. Seven hundred and twenty hours to sell $100 thousand worth of equipment. How much time do you have to spend on people that cannot help you do this? Get it?"

"Okay, I got you."

"Good." And that was it. He took another second to look me in the eye, winked and said, "Now get out of here, I do not have any more time to spend on you."

He got up with his paperwork and ran over to the printer to make copies of a contract he had just gotten signed. While he was taking the paperwork to be processed, I took the liberty of opening his appointment book and spying on his daily activities. What I saw shocked me.

Victor had his entire year planned out. He could look in his old leather appointment book and tell you what he would be doing eight or even nine months from that very day. Times to go to the gym, see parents, get breakfast, Monday morning meetings, golf dates with customers, weddings, St. Patrick's Day, New Years, Veterans Day, times to do work on the house, scheduled times to have drinks with his networking partners, dinner dates, holidays, vacations, were all given time slots in his daily planner. While I did what came to me in an improvisational manner, with Victor, nothing happened by chance.

As I walked past the only person in the company who could sell just as much, if not more than Victor, Mr. Kasseta's desk, I saw his appointment book was even thicker than Victor's. Years later, after I foolishly moved on and left Canon USA for what I believed was a better job, I heard through the grapevine that Doug and Victor had done what all top salespeople in companies do, they became president and CEOs by starting their own company.

After Victor's big speech, his words seemed to be haunting me. Every manager, director, CEO, president and small company owner I talked to was always going on and on about managing their time. "Please, do not waste my time or, "My time is short," or the most popular one, "I do not have time for this right now," was coming from every mouth in the rat race. This time thing was worthy of my respect and admiration. The more I paid attention to it, the more frightened of it I became.

Father time, precious time, times up, time out, in time, point in time, on time, just in the nick of time, timing, in due time, double time, time heals all wounds, time clock, no wine before its time, what time is it?, take your time---take your time, big time, timeless, make time for me, how much time do we have? real time, do not waste my time!, watch your time— watch your time, timed, out of time, how much time do we have left?, time!, time!, time!, let's spend some time together and my personal favorite, the time is now. They were time fearing people. Everyone except----me.

There were even expensive time management classes for the top executives that I thought were a complete waste of money as never once had anyone in college uttered a word to me about managing my time. But people in the rat race were obsessed with it. Time was the rat race. All the salespeople were wearing the most expensive watches on Earth trying to keep track of it. People either wanted more of it so they could make more money, or they needed more of it to spend it on their loved ones. The first sentence from the mouth of my first sales trainer was, "Time is your most valuable asset. If you do not keep track of it, you will never be a successful salesperson! If that's a problem for you, get another job."

Because we were selling computer and copier machines with the promise they would make a company more efficient, putting the company into instant overdrive, return on investment was on the lips of every salesman that was making a lot of money. All the CEOs wanted to know one thing, "What's my ROI? Meaning, how much time is it going to take for these computers and copiers to pay for themselves and then, start making me some serious money?"

They wanted the people working for them to do more work, in less time. If it took an accountant two weeks to file the company tax return and receive the check from Uncle Sam, they wanted our computers and copiers to help that accountant do the same amount of work in less than a week. They were watching time like a hawk. More work, done in less time meant one thing---- money, money, and more money. Using relationships to sell for me was like stealing time, while showing up to work late, was a formula for getting yourself fired.

As important as time was, you would have thought that at least one of my managers would have held a training class on how to spend it wisely. The companies only gave time management formulas to the important upper level managers, which I personally felt was a formula for sure failure for me. Well, luckily there was one man who owned a CPA firm I met that shared his formula for time management with me. It's simple so, I'll share it with you.

It describes what you should do and in what order. It says, do what is life and death first, what is critical second, important third, and what's not important last.

TIME MANAGEMENT MODEL

1st Life & Death	2nd Critical
3rd Important	4th Not Important

Taking the importance of time into consideration regarding financial success, *The Formula* changes just a little and becomes:

$$\frac{\textbf{Success} = (v)\text{Information} + (v)\text{Commodities} + (v)\text{Relationships}}{\textbf{Time}}$$

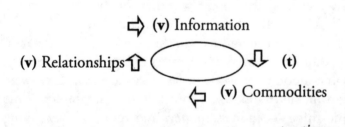

$t = time$

Once I realized how important all these things that I had never heard of in college were; things so important to making a money machine work without breaking down, my one and only question was, "Does anyone ever really need to go to college?"

MONEY IS THE POTENTIAL TO DO A MEASURED AMOUNT OF WORK, IN A MEASURED AMOUNT OF TIME.

THE FORMULA

DOING HARD TIME

&

25% of the US
population are college
educated

"THE GI BILL GAVE BIRTH TO THE LARGEST MIDDLE CLASS IN THE
HISTORY OF AMERICA."
- BARACK OBAMA – 44TH PRESIDENT OF THE UNITED STATES

The day my graduating class at Northeastern University was pulled into a long, well lit conference room and addressed by the Dean of the Electrical Engineering Department was a confusing one. It was supposed to be a happy day, but for some reason, he had a sullen look in his eyes. The same look you'd see from people at funerals.

He spoke to us with shame and disappointment in his tone. The tone of a man guilty of treason trying desperately to purge himself in confessional. I listened, fearing he was going to tell us our grades had been lost and we would have to take our exams over again to graduate. That would have been better than what he actually ended up saying.

76% of young Americans feel that a college degree is a necessity in their quest to get ahead in life

While the majority of the graduating class gave high fives and laughed with one another, he said, "I have to tell you the truth. This is only the beginning. You must continue your education as if your life depended on it. You must pursue a

234

master's and doctorate degree with the same intensity as you have used to acquire your bachelors." The only thing I could think of was, "WHAT? More school? Why didn't anyone tell me this before?" I felt betrayed. Just as I was about to feel happy and confident in my future, he showed up to pull the rug right out from under me.

The rejoicing in the room drowned out his words as few people listened. Too busy celebrating the great feat of graduation and all its wondrous financial hopes for the future I suppose. I heard him though. I knew that his words and tone meant painful, troubling times were up ahead. He was dancing around saying outright that the degree of information we were so proud of was not going to protect us like the force field we had been told it would. I should have known it was too good to be true.

For others who had parents with the means to support them for another two years of school, it was truly only the beginning. But for me, a young man with a mother who desperately needed him to get a high paying job as quickly as possible, it was like going over a waterfall with no life jacket. I worried for myself, but even more, I worried for my mother. How was I ever going to explain this to her?

When I got out into the rat race, under pressure to make as much money as possible, I put additional school time out of my mind. It just was not an option for me. All the successful basketball players and musicians who had dropped out of college to become millionaires did not have master's degrees, so they became my role models. Besides, I was an engineer. The worshiped creator of all creation. It could not be any harder than some of the classes I had just escaped from with my life. Come what may, I would find a way.

My degree was so important to everyone I met though. Every time I got around my parents friends, they always asked, "What did you study in school Son?" It was as if I was no longer a person. I was just my degree. It earned me all the social accolades amongst my mother's friends, just less the financial ones. After a while, I began to resent my degree.

This resentment was further cemented when I watched a historian explain the history of college and its origins in a documentary on Ancient Egyptian civilization. Apparently, early civilizations reserved higher learning only for the kings and queens and their children. Once they were of appropriate age, they were shipped off to colleges of the highest reputation to be educated and "cultured". This process was not for the purpose of acquiring a job or some practical skill. The pain of this process was endured only in an effort to make the young aristocrat appear more presentable and noble in the eyes of their peers and other heads of state.

> *70% of the fastest growing professions in the US require a college degree to be considered for hire*

Watching stories about famous businesspeople on television just made matters worse. Tommy Hilfiger said, "I hated school and could not wait to get out and start my own business." Tom Cruise was never formally trained in acting school. Bill Gates is a college dropout. Henry Ford began his journey in the automotive industry at age 16. Steve Jobs left college after one semester to change the world of computers and Mary Kay Ash skipped college for a career in cosmetics and now, half a million women are selling Mary Kay throughout the world.

> *4 out of 5 of the richest men in the world were college dropouts*

Richard Branson dropped out of school at age 16 and went on to achieve success in everything from magazines to music. Coco Chanel went from being an orphan to become an icon in fashion. Michael Dell dropped out of college at age 19 and used $1000 to re-invent the world of computers. Walt Disney dropped out of school at 19 to control the world of animated movies. After a while, it became clear, in my young naive eyes at least, that college was just another sales pitch to sell a commodity called information.

This college degree product just was not working. Too many of my friends who had bought them were still in serious financial pain. I was being beaten up by the rat race in far worse a fashion than what the Untouchables had done to me. I felt like asking for a refund.

It was not just the top levels of wealth, fame and power that were building a case against college. I met families from the poorest countries on Earth who had worked together and now owned laundromats, and fruit stands all over New York City. They were living nothing short of the good life while I, equipped with my college degree, was struggling just to survive.

To add insult to injury, I met a man selling hot dogs on the corner who had a house in Garden City Long Island worth $2 million. These simple people were making a mockery and a fool out of my efforts. Then, just as I was about to lose complete and total trust in college as a product, I heard a term that stopped me in my tracks. The term was critical thinking.

I was on another one of my many interviewing experiences. The gentleman interviewing me said, "Well, what do you bring to this position?" Not knowing how to respond, I pulled my ready-made response out and gave it to him like an actor recites his lines on stage.

"Well, I have an electrical engineer degree from Northeastern University and I have had a few summer jobs as a technician that gives me some experience in the business world." He must have already heard that reply because he cut me right off.

"Listen. I tell all the candidates the same thing. College is only good for two things. It tells me for one, you can begin a difficult task and then see it through to the end.

The second thing it says to me is, maybe, just maybe, you might be able to think critically and make smart choices. The hope of you being able to do this is what got you into that seat in front of me. What you say now might get you

> *Only 10% of the richest people in the world do not have college degrees*

the job." I sat there stunned as no one had ever been so blunt with me before. Through his harsh demeanor, somehow, it felt as if he was trying to help me, as well as himself.

"Do you have any idea how many people I have had to hire and then fire because they say they are going to do the world once they get the job and in the end, they cannot complete the simplest of tasks? Don't even think about asking them to make a decision on something. If you ask them, we have pencils and pens to choose from. Which ones should we pick, they can't make a choice. They're stumped. I can't hire people like that on my team. I need people that can think on their feet. Make the right choice if I am not around. Can you do that Mr. Powell?" I sat there stunned and as you may have already guessed, I did not get the job. But, I got something else far more valuable. Finally, I saw value in my college degree other than being a conversation piece at parties.

Although a number of the most successful people in the world of wealth, fame and power were college or even worse, high school dropouts, without fail, every single person they hired or trusted to run their precious money machines were full of degrees from the best schools in the land. The only time an exception to that formula for success was made, was if the person was a salesman.

My entire scholastic career had all been to teach me how to think. How to think critically to be specific. How to compare two or more things and then, make a choice about how to create or sell a new--thing. One that would be a combination of the first two, yet new, fresh and exciting. Once I finally had *The Formula* in my palm, I realized that if information, commodities and relationships were indeed the keys to success, there was **NO** better place in the world to acquire them than in college.

Just like the cartoons of my childhood that would test me to compare three dogs and identify the one with its tongue hanging out, college was there to teach me how to make choices about the differences between things and then, how to make the choice that would steer me through the middle of the two of them to the land of success.

College taught those like me, those that did not have successful role models in their homes teaching us how to do it; how not to make poor choices. How to be a successful CEO. A great president. A top level decision maker.

College stuffed a ridiculous amount of formulas into my brain and then forced me to compare and contrast them to various situations to see if I would make the right choice in the form of-----a test. As simple as this may sound, decision making skill are the single most overlooked cause of financial failure for people throughout the world. This ability to think critically is the difference between success and failure, wealth or poverty, and in many cases, life or death.

Money managers, responsible for the safety and growth of millions, sometimes billions of dollars must apply critical thinking skills every hour of every day. The choice to buy one company as opposed to another can result in millions and at times, billions of dollars in losses. A buyer for a clothing store must apply critical thinking skills when choosing to stock one designers clothing over another. A grocery store owner must do the same thing as shelf space is limited, and the wrong commodities on shelves can make or break his store. The CEO of a record company must apply critical thinking when choosing which musical artist to market and promote. The wrong choice can destroy the company's profits in a matter of months.

The importance of critical thinking to make my money machine work, as much as I did not want to accept it, was too valuable to ignore. For a time there, I was obsessed with it. So obsessed, I actually considered going back to school for a master's degree. I wondered, "What sort of hoops do you have to jump through to get one of those things?"

THE ABILITY TO THINK CRITICALLY IS FAR MORE IMPORTANT THAN PHYSICAL STRENGTH.

KNOWLEDGE CANNOT BE MERELY A DEGREE OR A SKILL. IT DEMANDS A BROADER VISION, CAPABILITIES IN CRITICAL THINKING, WITHOUT WHICH WE CANNOT HAVE PROGRESS.
- LI KA SHING--RICHEST MAN IN CHINA

THE MASTER

৪১

> "I BELIEVE THE TRUE ROAD TO PREEMINENT SUCCESS IN ANY LINE IS
> TO MAKE YOURSELF MASTER IN THAT LINE. I HAVE NO FAITH IN THE
> POLICY OF SCATTERING ONE'S RESOURCES, AND IN MY EXPERIENCE
> I HAVE RARELY IF EVER MET A MAN WHO ACHIEVED PREEMINENCE
> IN MONEY MAKING... CERTAINLY NEVER ONE IN MANUFACTURING...
> WHO WAS INTERESTED IN MANY CONCERNS."
> - ANDREW CARNEGIE

When I told my mother I was starting a publishing company and would be writing books instead of being the engineer from now on, without blinking an eye she said, "Sure you are Bintell. You will get tired of it and put it with all your other unfinished projects." Before I could say, "No Mom, I am serious about this," she replied, "This so-called book, the one you have not written yet, will end up underneath something at the bottom of your closet as soon as the first wind blows your attention onto something else more exciting I am sure." Well, she had a point. Over the years, I have managed to develop a reputation as a jack-of-all-trades, yet a master of not even one.

There was a short-lived, yet promising career as a baseball pitcher where somehow, I was able to take my team right to the championship game. Unfortunately the next season, I abandoned baseball completely because my dad did not have time to drive me to practice. Less than a year later, after working hard to develop a reputation as the fastest defensive player in the league, my promising soccer career ended for the same reason. Only this time, in the years that followed, I had the pleasure of watching friends I was better than, become so talented, they left me behind making the Olympic Team and traveling the world.

Then there was my time as the best table tennis player in my neighborhood that evaporated into thin air. There was another short lived football career in Texas and a fascination with boxing care of The Untouchables and my good friend Ben. Another short stint as a clothing designer, and let us not forget a passion for drawing lions and tigers all day in a hypnotic trance that somehow too, went the way of the wind. And last but definitely not least, my beloved yet abandoned musical career. Oh yes, even though Mom's words hurt my feelings more than a bit, I had to admit, she did have a valid point. The truth is, the only thing I have ever stuck with for a decent amount of time, is being a salesman, and that's probably because of money.

The worst part about my on again, off again passionate dates with success was, the time I wasted. If I spent six years developing my talent in music, only to abandon it because the pain of continuing was in my eyes more than the pleasure of the success it would bring, the break in continuity was like a huge hole in my life. Like all I had done in that time had never happened. Well, thank goodness it was not a total waste of time. Somehow I managed to take away a simple message from all those cancelled dates with success which was, the more formulas, the merrier.

In literature, there are formulas called literary devices that masterful writers choose from to produce different emotional effects for the reader. These devices are used in the same way I watched my mother picked colors from her coloring box to paint a perfect picture, only these devices have the same effect on the senses with words. Salesman like Victor and Doug had 10 different methods of bringing a meeting from a conversation to a signed contract they could use on any given day. As a young

SUCCESS = I + C + R

pitcher, I had about 10 pitches in my back pocket I could pick from to ensure a strikeout, no matter how tight a squeeze I found myself in.

As a wanna-be neighborhood table tennis champion, I had the same amount of ways to serve or return the ball as I did pitches in baseball. Sometimes with a spin, sometimes fast and with a spin, sometimes with a lob, or even still, sometimes with an elusive bounce back towards me. Having and using them gave me the same sense of calm and security as pulling aces out of my pocket in a card game.

More than half of my life was spent memorizing a very healthy amount of formulas in music and when Ben, my semi-professional boxing buddy brought me to his basement to show me a few tricks of his boxing trade, he too had a surplus of jabs, upper cuts from various angles using either hand, combinations mixed with footwork designed to ensure success in a fight as quickly as possible, with the least amount of risk of bodily harm. Watching him divulge all his secrets told me one thing, "Ben doesn't even know how to lose!"

From musicians, to painters, to athletes, straight ahead to salespeople, there was a common theme with all of them; they had a million ways to get it, success that is.

Every successful person I have ever admired or looked up to, and wanted desperately to copy and paste their success right into my own life, was secretly relying on more than just one formula for success they could pick from their hip pocket at will, for each and every situation they could ever find themselves in. Formulas were the keys to success in just about everything yes, but having more than just one to choose from in any situation, made you more than just successful, it made you a master.

Boxers, tennis players, musicians, chefs, writers, artist, stockbrokers, actors, salesman, the great ones at least, the masters, were all stuffed to capacity with formulas and models for

243

success. If mastery is your goal, having about 10 or so formulas that guaranteed success in any and every situation should be first on your list of things to do, starting----now.

Trust me when I tell you, the people who have already mastered *The Formula* will do one of two things. They will either develop a relationship with you as a friend, or they will use this formula with no mercy to eliminate you as the competition and achieve the success they believe is their birthright. The worst of them are called mercenaries. They are people that will do **anything** for money. In their eyes, this game of wealth, fame and power is nothing short of war. They will use every piece of information, any commodity and any and all relationships at their disposal to win. Don't ever forget that!

One last thing, the most valuable commodity you will ever create, and then recreate is you. This is the key to everything. You are your own best formula!

And now, I am happy to say, you are free to go. Go on, get out of here. You are not finished learning, but you do know enough to defend yourself against the best the top 9 percent will throw at you. So get in the game as fast as you can. You have spent enough time here with me. Go make all your dreams and more come true. Once you have reached Success Blvd., if you do not have time to write, please, when your neighbors ask you, "What do you do?" meaning, how in God's name did you sift through all that information we sent at you and get here, lean over and tell them the same way my friend with the candy store told me. Tell them you rode into town in a money machine called, *The Formula*.

SUCCESS = I + C + R

SUCCESS IS SOMETHING THAT TURNS OUT AS PLANNED.

SUCCESS IS A POINT IN TIME WHERE PREPARATION & OPPORTUNITY COLLIDE.

SUCCESS IS THE ATTAINMENT OF WEALTH, FAME & POWER.

SUCCESS IS A CHOICE TO SUCCEED.

SUCCESS IS YOUR BIRTHRIGHT. BE WHAT YOU HAVE COME HERE FOR!

MAKE YOUR MACHINE

&

Use these last pages to create your own money machine. Use a pencil because as you know, the only thing predictable in business, is the unpredictability of change.

Have fun!

Success =

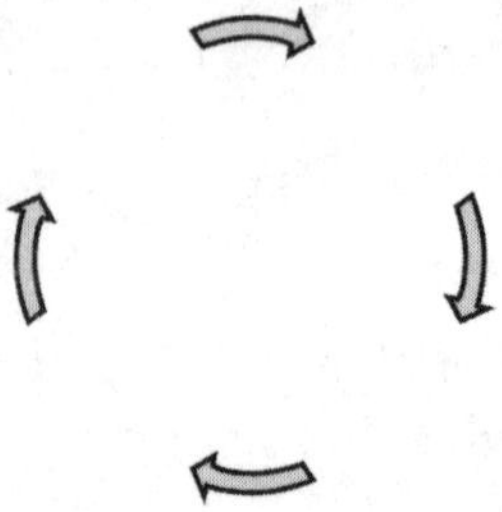

⟶

↑   ↓

⟵

Success =

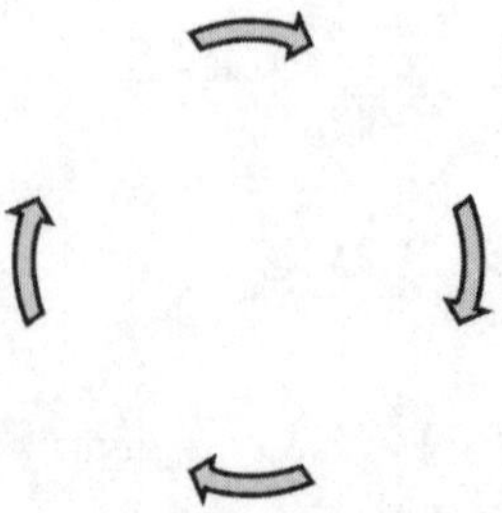

⟶

↑   ↓

⟵

SUCCESS = I + C + R

Success =

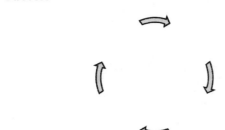

Success =

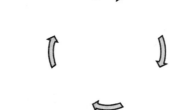

Success =

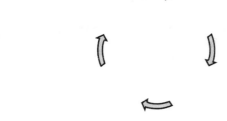

Success =

Success =

Success =

Success =

Success =